A Teacher's Guide to Anger Management

Anger is a daily feature of school life. It is a fact of life that often gets in the way of the teaching process for both pupils and their teachers. Yet very little training or time has been given to one of the biggest blocks to school improvement.

This book presents a recognisable and truthful account of this widespread problem and sets out to help teachers understand more about anger in practical terms. It suggests simple strategies for dealing with angry individuals in the classroom and outlines more complex longer-term solutions that can be developed in schools and used as part of a PSHE programme on Assertive Behaviour.

This book will give teachers the knowledge and confidence to deal with angry individuals and aggressive situations.

Paul Blum is Head of Learning Support at an inner-city school and was involved with the Everyman project on anger management. He is the author of the best-selling *Surviving and Succeeding in Difficult Classrooms*, also published by RoutledgeFalmer.

This book was written in the author's free time and the views expressed represent the views of the author. They are not based on any particular school, and do not represent the views of any particular school.

A Teacher's Guide to Anger Management

Paul Blum

London and New York

First published 2001 by RoutledgeFalmer
11 New Fetter Lane, London EC4P 4EE

Simultaneously published in the USA and Canada
by RoutledgeFalmer
29 West 35th Street, New York, NY 10001

RoutledgeFalmer is an imprint of the Taylor & Francis Group

© 2001 Paul Blum

Typeset in Palatino by
Keystroke, Jacaranda Lodge, Wolverhampton
Printed and bound in Great Britain by TJ International Ltd,
Padstow, Cornwall

British Library Cataloguing-in-Publication Data
A catalogue record for this book is available from the British Library

Library of Congress Cataloging in Publication Data
Blum, Paul.
    A teacher's guide to anger management/Paul Blum.
        p.cm.
    ISBN 0–415–23198–1 (pbk.)
    1. Classroom management. 2. Anger. I. Title
LB3013 .B55 2001
371.102′4–dc21   00–054290

Contents

Acknowledgements

I would like to thank the following people for making it possible for me to write this book:

Valerie Coultas for her practical ideas. Jim Finn, Roger Koester and other members of the anger management group at the Everyman project in Stockwell.

Also to Steve Potter, John Hudson, Deirdre Murphy, Chris Hardy and Tim Ball for their help and support in the autumn of 1998 when life was very difficult for me.

Introduction

Educational bureaucracy currently points to the need to drive up standards with better quality teaching as the way to solve the problem of disaffection and underachievement in schools. It has done some commendable work on identifying literacy and numeracy as vital key skills that every teacher needs to improve their teaching of. But improved teaching, while a vital strategy in reducing the incidents of verbal or physical abuse, is only one part of a much more comprehensive programme needed to tackle the underlying causes of anger, low motivation and abusive behaviour in our schools. Historically, the vast majority of teachers are inventive and resourceful at finding their way around a whole lot of behaviour problems. However, they could be given more help with the positive work that they do.

If the right questions are not asked, the right answers cannot be found. This book looks at how relationships and gender identities play their role in the build-up of anger and tension in the system. It is honest about what is going wrong and how it can be improved upon.

The majority of scenarios that this book looks at are boy dominated because the overriding evidence is that the vast majority of dangerous and abusive pupils are boys. As Part 3 of the book shows, intervention strategies to help pupils contain their anger look at how feelings can be expressed without resorting to verbal or physical abuse. Showing feelings seems to be more difficult for male pupils than female pupils. Perhaps not surprisingly it is boys who predominate in the anger management intervention strategies that I exemplify in this book.

Part 1

On how anger is causing problems to pupils and teachers in our schools

Chapter 1

A survey of anger situations that teachers face in schools

How many of the following situations happen in the lessons you teach? Around the corridors in the school at lunchtime? Between lessons? After the day is over at the bus stop or train station? If the answer to the vast majority is 'never', then this book will be of no more than academic interest to you. If the answer is 'frequently' or 'occasionally', then you might find it useful to read on. If the answer is 'no' for most of the pupils but 'yes' for a significant hard-core minority, then this book could be useful to you.

IN THE CLASSROOM

1 A pupil deliberately bumps into another in the classroom. There is a bit of pushing, shoving and name calling.
2 A pupil flings an object such as a paper plane or screwed-up paper ball across your classroom. Another student flings something back. A round of flinging paper begins and it is difficult to get your lesson back on track.
3 A pupil cusses another across the room. It seems to start as a joke but it starts to get out of hand. Lesson momentum is seriously interrupted.
4 A pupil takes another pupil's bag or pen and refuses to give it back.
5 A number of pupils mock and insult each other in a round

of energetic banter during the lesson. As a result a lot of working time is lost.

6 Two pupils are having a stand-up argument in your class. They incite each other to a fight. The class shouts and jeers encouragement.

7 A pupil gets in a strop at being told off. They verbally abuse you.

8 A pupil gets in a temper when they are told to concentrate on the lesson. They kick their chair or a table.

9 A pupil shows you disrespect with an obscene mouth gesture, nicknamed 'kissing the teeth'. The rest of the class laugh.

10 A pupil is asked to leave the room and goes out kicking over a desk or a chair, and maybe slamming a door.

11 You have a fully fledged fight in the classroom.

12 A pupil keeps on interrupting you and becomes verbally abusive when you ask them to stop doing it.

13 You may be in a situation in which a pupil needs to be stopped from getting up to hit another pupil in your classroom.

14 A pupil pushes past you. They refuse to stay for their detention.

OUTSIDE THE CLASSROOM

1 Pupils who are not in your lesson keep on trying to get into your classroom to speak to a friend. They are verbally confrontational and try to push past you.

2 Pupils get into a large group and chase another group of pupils down the corridor, shouting abuse at them and then attempting to attack them.

3 A huge group of pupils, almost the entire school population, run across the playground to get a ringside view of a fight.

4 An entourage of pupils encourage two pupils to fight.

5 There is a violent incident at the local bus stop between your

school and the one down the road. The police are called. You are trying to go home at the time.

6 Strangers to the school try to enter to settle a feud with a pupil in your building. Their behaviour is aggressive and they are intent on physical violence.

7 Pupils are involved in physical horseplay as they move between lessons. There is a lot of pushing, shoving and jeering.

8 Pupils are shouting at each other as they move slowly between their lessons.

9 An angry parent comes up to the school. You see them shouting and making threats.

10 You ask a pupil to leave the room. They swear at you and refuse to budge.

You may have seen some or all of these things happening in your school.

TEENAGERS' BEHAVIOUR

The teenagers involved in aggressive displays are often play-acting. They are testing out physical and mental boundaries through the rough and tumble of their interactions with each other and the teachers. Many of the events are playful and harmless but a significant minority that start like this quickly degenerate into disruptive aggressive situations. The 11- to 18-year old youngsters involved are at an age when egos are much more insecure and fragile than in fully fledged adults. What starts out as a bit of fun can quickly upset or offend. The banter of physical and verbal abuse that the pupils engage in is a dangerous and volatile activity, and the culture of aggressive display (which we look at in more detail later in the book) is also an ingrained part of youngsters' lives. This makes the boundaries of what is acceptable and unacceptable more easily blurred. A form of street culture is a norm reference for so many social interactions with its brash aggressive posturings. One look at playground behaviour for boys supports this. Most boys conform to a stereotype in which they run about playing football. The only emotions that are deemed expressible are demonstrated in pushing, tugging, slapping on the back and mock fighting. This book will show that the limitations in the range of emotions that boys are allowed to show make aggressive angry behaviour all the more likely. The effects of this on the whole school community will be discussed later.

Many incidents on the initial lists you were asked to consider could occur with less frequency in secondary schools if tired and frustrated teachers did not encourage escalation, by responding to such unruly and aggressive behaviour in kind. In some circumstances they will shout first, shout back, overreact, provoke and escalate situations further. Sometimes this happens because the teachers themselves are part of a macho aggressive culture in which some of their professional colleagues bully the students and gain quick obedience from them. This can put pressure on *all* teachers to perform in a certain way, to command, shout down and dominate, or else be seen as weak and ineffective.

A school is meant to be a place where the main activities are teaching and learning. For those two activities to take place successfully, certain things are critical. The school must have a stable emotional environment. A teacher cannot teach classes of between twenty and thirty individuals effectively unless there is a calm, purposeful equilibrium. All teachers need to know how to control themselves and the anger of their pupils if a lesson is to stay on course.

HOW COULD THIS BOOK HELP YOU?

This book sets out to help teachers understand more about the causes of the anger that leads to verbal abuse and violence every day in their workplace. It focuses on the laddish culture that surrounds teachers in school and society as a whole and the way it impinges on relationships and expectations in the classroom.

This book gives practical advice about what you can do to minimise and control the anger of your pupils in difficult situations. It explains the ways you could influence your school to move forward as an institution on anger management so that all relationships within it can improve and classrooms can become a better place for learning. It is hoped that the strategies suggested here would also be useful to all support staff who have to deal with angry pupils.

The advice comes at a time when teaching unions are reporting increased frequency of teachers experiencing physical and verbal abuse from their pupils. Despite this alarming situation, the vast majority of teachers are able to find incredibly creative ways of forming positive relationships with their most challenging pupils. This book should help to sustain them in their work by showing new approaches to handling angry behaviours as well as reinforcing the approaches they already use.

Chapter 2

The conflicts of managing behaviour in schools

INCLUSION, EXCLUSION AND THE LACK OF REAL CONSENSUS ON HOW TO HANDLE POOR BEHAVIOUR

If you asked teachers what their greatest frustration is, the majority will tell you about the anxieties they have over the behaviour of a few individual pupils in their class. Teachers worry about how these pupils' behaviour will impinge on all the other pupils. Everyday they use much more of their nervous energy anticipating how the behaviour of a few will spoil their lessons than on improving the way that they teach the majority of well-motivated pupils.

If you asked the educational bureaucrats who work for the local education authorities (LEAs) and the Department for Education and Employment (DfEE) what they are most concerned about within the British school system, they may concentrate on what is described as the quality of the teaching and learning, particularly in basic skills. Although this includes the issue of behaviour management it often seems that it is by no means their main focus and priority. The bureaucrats, after all, are not the ones who have to manage the behaviour of twenty-five or more teenagers in each lesson and they constantly underestimate how difficult it is to do this well. Perhaps they don't understand how pivotal it is to the teacher's daily experience of the classroom.

The government and the LEAs have recently focused on the policy of social and educational inclusion for all pupils in all schools. It has not been a problem to explain why pupils with physical, visual and hearing impairments should be integrated into mainstream schools. I have been to conferences where there hasn't been a murmur from the headteachers on this policy apart from worrying about the accessibility of their school buildings. But mention the words emotional behavioural difficulty (EBD) and there is a big sigh in the room. There is a great fear of this, the biggest group of Special Needs pupils. Heads and their staff may be worried by the challenges they offer. Parents and governors may feel their schools have enough behaviour problems to deal with already. They may be frightened of the aspect of an inclusion policy that threatens to make it harder to exclude pupils temporarily and permanently. Almost unanimously they ask how they are supposed to improve results and at the same time absorb even greater numbers of challenging pupils who can often spoil lessons.

Some schools have been given money under the Excellence in Cities (EiC) initiative to set up behaviour support units. The government intends that these units should be used as a temporary measure to help pupils who are having behavioural problems in mainstream classes. But some schools have been using them as a way of getting difficult and uncooperative students out of the system for a few weeks to give their teachers and the rest of the pupils a breather.

In the Education Action Zones the National Curriculum can be disapplied to let some pupils pursue courses personally tailored for their needs. Some schools have used this as a way of creating classes with behaviourally challenging pupils and removing them from the main system. They are being tucked away in the quiet corners of buildings so they can be contained without disturbing others.

None of this is in keeping with the spirit of inclusion but many schools are frightened of children with EBDs. The great majority of the staff have not been trained to deal with behaviourally challenging pupils whether the school has them in large or small numbers. So if the LEAs are cutting back on off-site provision for children with EBDs, many schools will be increasingly tempted to create on-site provision which is like a school within a school – a 'sin bin' in which to shove difficult problems.

Currently it seems that there isn't an honest and open dialogue between schools and policy-makers about how best to deal with pupil anger and disaffection. Without an honest dialogue, real progress on these issues is difficult. Central government simply imposes its own solutions to these problems and then links its own initiatives to funding that schools desperately need. There are few hurdles they won't jump in a bid to get a little extra money.

TEACHERS DIVIDED ON BEHAVIOUR MANAGEMENT

Any honest dialogue on behaviour would reveal that there is little consensus about the best way of managing it. No two people agree exactly about managing behaviour. Individual teachers find their own personal way of maintaining good order in the classroom and that takes years of experience. There are usually several camps on behaviour management in the staff of a typical school. Into these camps fit a range of individual styles.

DOMINANT TEACHERS

The first camp is the dominant one: their position is that 'I am a teacher and I'm here to teach. As I'm in charge of the classroom, pupils will do what I tell them to do. Pupils who have a particular problem with that should not be in my classroom.' This end of the staff room is usually in favour of punishment and sanction as the cure to the problems of particular pupils. Dominant teachers want exclusion and expulsion if other sanctions don't work. They are sceptical about rewards, believing they pander to low student expectations.

System reward teachers

A small subgroup of system sanction teachers is system reward teachers. They are more accessible to the idea of rewards to manipulate behaviour in a positive direction. They are happy to use rewards flexibly and imaginatively.

SPECIALIST BEHAVIOURAL INTERVENTION

Most specialist behavioural intervention work with challenging pupils lays stress on flexible approaches to behaviour, with the emphasis on rewards outstripping sanctions. But the dominant disciplinarians don't need the systems of either rewards or sanctions to enforce their egos on a class to get them 'under manners'. They often find the routines of systematic rewarding and punishing too tedious to administer. The systems people who usually feel more comfortable using sanctions to grind their pupils' resistance down also believe that positive rewards are ineffectual. They usually subscribe to the view that human nature understands the punishment scenario much more readily.

THE DOMINANT TEACHING PHILOSOPHY ON BEHAVIOUR

Whatever the school handbooks say about positive rewarding for good behaviour, in practice it is the negative philosophies that have often gained the moral high ground in mainstream schooling. It is often personalities from the emphatic disciplinarian group that have gained the dominant role – being promoted into high positions because they can control pupils and command obedience. But their approach does not help the majority of teachers who play neither of the above extreme roles that well, yet often feel highly pressurised into copying one of the above styles, with embarrassingly poor results.

'Drama and personality' discipline teachers

Within the dominant teachers' group are the high-energy 'impulse' disciplinarians. They don't like systems of reward or sanctions but instead use the power of their personality to overcome difficult situations.

'Sit there now! You do exactly as you are told or you'll be sorry.'

'Get over there now. Sit down and shut up!'

There is a lot of drama around the enforcing of egos. These teachers' displays are often entertaining and exciting. They are often highly liked and respected individuals. By equal measure many are disliked and feared. But the principles on which their discipline is based is not flexible. Pupils who react aggressively to a barracking from such teachers and answer back rather than submit to their domination soon reach a point of no return. The only alternative to this is to be excluded.

This style of laddish discipline is the dominant style of behavioural management in many secondary schools and boys' schools.

SYSTEM SANCTION TEACHERS

The second broad category of opinion and style in schools contains the systems people. They impose their personality on their classes *not* through dominant ego displays but by strong enforcement of school systems or, when those are lacking, their own personal ones. Often the emphasis is on sanction, with members of this group manipulating pupils into behaving rather than blasting them out with theatrics. These teachers wear the pupils down with systems.

How effective is the dominant philosophy with EBD pupils?

Neither dominant groups have any answer to the problems of the emotional behaviourally challenging pupils with their mood swings and unpredictable outbursts of rage. The inflexible sanction-led approach soon means that this minority of pupils falls foul of the system again and again.

The only inclusive way forward for many of these pupils would be flexible behaviour management strategies based on positive rewards and a lot of tolerance about what constitutes little steps of good progress. But in the system where the teacher is always right and where the accepted codes of behaviour form a very rigid norm, confrontation is almost inevitable and the frequency of pupils becoming verbally and physically abusive becomes correspondingly higher.

The path of compromise

Headteachers of schools often have to tread very difficult paths of compromise and fudge between the wishes of powerful and seemingly conflicting interest groups. On the one side are teachers who want stern sanctions and many permanent exclusions. On the other side are LEAs and government, which want a reduction in exclusions and more effective inclusion for difficult pupils. There are not only parents who want strict discipline but also parents who feel that their children are not being given a fair chance. There is the contradiction of a school wanting to improve exam results by increasing the number of lessons which are orderly and well structured, yet at the same time being told to keep more and more disaffected pupils in those very mainstream classes they are seeking to improve.

A better way forward on behaviour

Clearly there is a real need for all teachers to receive proper training in how to be effective managers of behaviour. To do this they need carefully constructed training throughout their teaching careers. Schools themselves need to introduce more flexible systems to manage challenging behaviour which have a genuine reward-based culture at their heart. At the moment many don't have faith in a rewards culture and fall back on a punishment culture with all its side-effects.

The current policy for inclusion looks set to stay, whether teachers like it or not. Before it existed there were always angry and emotionally volatile pupils. All teachers need to look more carefully at how they respond personally to the difficulties of dealing with abusive angry youngsters. In the real world of the classroom they are not going to go away.

We would have a more effective response to the problems presented by angry demotivated pupils if the majority of teachers concentrated more on system rewards and stopped using ungainly and unconvincing bullying or constant punishment. This idea will be explored in the following chapters of this book.

Chapter 3

Teacher stress in managing behaviour

WHY DO TEACHERS GET ANGRIER THAN THEY NEED TO?

Teachers, like pupils, can get sucked into the anger/confrontation spiral in schools. Like angry pupils, they can miss their warning signals and pass the moment of danger. Just like the pupils, this is far more likely to happen when they are stressed, tired or hungry.

Teachers' anger will often be triggered by the same feelings as some of their more challenging pupils:

- fear
- panic
- a sense of inadequacy
- embarrassment
- insecurity
- frustration
- a feeling of belittlement

TEACHER ANGER: THE HIDDEN AGENDA OF WATCHING AND BEING WATCHED

There are many different teaching styles present in a school but two seem to have more status than others: those who bark orders successfully and those who punish bad behaviour with tenacious sanction systems. The key thing about both groups is that they appear to be getting an instantaneous response from the pupils. When these teachers ask classes to be quiet, they are. When they admonish pupils in the corridor, they stand still and don't back chat. When they walk into a classroom, pupils go silent. And this seems to happen in schools in the most difficult locations as well, though perhaps the time delay of response is a little greater; the dressing downs last a little longer and occur more frequently, but in essence the same happens.

Although schools are meant to be centred on teaching and learning, they are also focused on power, authority and social control. Having the pupils obedient and compliant carries a separate kudos all of its own. Heads who don't have it usually want to appoint teachers who do high into the hierarchy as an insurance policy. Heads who do have it see themselves in other younger prodigies and promote their self-image. Sometimes these teachers are also excellent in the classroom and command real respect, but often they are not, ruling instead by fear and bullying.

The way these teachers strut about enforcing law and order with the wag of a finger and the bark of a command unnerves their professional colleagues – the vast majority of the teaching staff. In turn, less dominant teachers often feel pressured into responding to the pupils in a more aggressive power-seeking way than they would otherwise have done. The majority use more sanctions than rewards. They get into more regular confrontation than is personally sensible for them because they want to be seen as getting instant respect from the pupils. If they are being watched by a number of pupils or another teacher, their reaction is even more extreme. Being confronted by an individual pupil in front of a whole class will often make a teacher act more aggressively. Being observed by a colleague will usually make a teacher feel even more inclined to try to assert their authority in a no nonsense way.

So within the profession itself there is a hidden competition and a sense of watching and being watched. How quickly do the pupils respond to your comments? How quickly can you get them to be quiet? How long can you keep it like that? Most daily judgements of colleagues are formed by fleeting glimpses of their style and not by sitting in on their lessons every day. The majority of teachers would deny that such internal competition on behaviour management exists. They would claim that they are not interested in using the macho style discipline that is seen to get such instant effects. But often they flounder into it with ungainly results when they feel embarrassed and ashamed by their colleagues seeing them struggling for control. Their aggression in these situations increases the volatility of the school. In the same way as there is posturing and real anger between the pupils and between pupils and teachers, so there is also pressure between teachers to adopt confrontational postures towards pupils. In these ways the dynamics for anger in classrooms – and schools – are set up.

TEACHER ANGER AND THE EXPECTATIONS OF THE SYSTEM

Teacher anger is brought on by other forms of stress, particularly from the way that the education system is set up. Most importantly, there is the blunt fact that a substantial minority of pupils in compulsory education aged 11 to 16 are fed up with being cooped up behind a desk all day. They may well be behind in terms of basic literacy and numeracy skills. They have had years of feeling inadequate at handling the academic curriculum. Day after day, lesson after lesson behind a desk reinforces their feelings of inadequacy, leaving them unstimulated and uncooperative. The system fails to redress this and remotivate them, because there is a standardised curriculum for teachers to deliver and standardised exams for pupils to sit.

The disillusionment and failure of these pupils often surface as anger, stimulating insecurity and low self-esteem in the teachers struggling to keep them motivated in lessons. The teachers become angry and confrontational with their disaffected pupils, which is hardly surprising as teachers and pupils alike are being asked to wade through the situation together.

DEMANDS ON TEACHERS FROM OUTSIDE THE SCHOOL

The external expectations of the DfEE and the Office for Standards in Education (OfSTED) are also piled onto the headteachers of schools. These can be somewhat unrealistic: the transformation of literacy and numeracy levels, huge increases in academic success in the General Certificate of Seconday Education (GCSE) and fewer problem pupils excluded from school. Heads pass the pressures down the line and thereby raise levels of stress and anger in their staff.

The teachers feel squeezed between the educational system from above and the difficulties with truculent and disaffected teenage pupils from below. They may sometimes feel they are not getting effective backup from their headteachers. The daily reality of the classrooms that teachers endure is a very different world from the one in which the Whitehall target-setters scheme the transformation of the British education system.

Power in education rests with those outside the schools and often leaves the professionals inside them feeling angry and powerless. The contradictions of the system contribute seriously to the mixed-up emotions and feelings of rage that many teachers find themselves with.

WHAT SORTS OF STRESS ARE TEACHERS EXPERIENCING?

Teachers often tell me that they feel isolated. They feel the burden of expectations coming from the educational bureaucracy. They feel the tremendous weight of unruly and restless behaviour coming from a significant minority of pupils. They feel inadequate knowing that they are judged by their ability to quell the pupils and find it a constant and exhausting battle.

They often feel they are failing. Few schools have systems for helping teachers to control the pupils better. Staff are often struggling on their own to keep their heads above water. They are not easing each other's load. They are often afraid to say just how hard they are finding it, for fear of being ridiculed as soft and therefore incompetent.

The next chapter looks in more detail at the evolution of the culture of schooling, based around stereotyped masculine values, that makes the business of educating such a frustrating experience for so many professionals.

Chapter 4

The educational world and macho

Since the late 1990s the educational world has started to take the issue of boys' underachievement very seriously. A number of articles have commented on boys' attitudes to learning at school. These have reminded us of what we already suspected, that self-styled hard, macho images do not help boys to learn. Laddism has stopped them getting on with their studies and meant they were more inclined to lark about in class. Many pieces of research during the 1990s identified boys' laddish behaviour in front of their mates as spoiling their concentration in lessons.

I believe that the macho laddish culture has a fundamental effect on the whole learning atmosphere for **all pupils** both in and outside their classrooms. In this chapter I shall examine what effect macho has on the learning environment. I believe that understanding macho is the key to understanding where anger and conflict come from in schools.

STORIES ILLUSTRATING THE NUANCES OF MACHO CULTURE

Anger at the swimming pool

A teenage boy complains to the attendant about his 20 pence getting stuck in the changing-room clothes locker. The problem has occurred because he has put in two 10 pence coins. The attendant tells him that he must get his money back from the main desk. The teenage boy (about 14) is not pleased with the answer. He does not like the tone of voice in which he is spoken to, nor the fact that the attendant does not even bother to get up from his seat.

But then he did not phrase his request to get the 10 pence coins back in a very articulate way. He cannot respond by telling the man how he feels about the way he has just treated him. **Saying how you feel is not part of the macho tradition.** Instead he bangs his fist on a locker as he walks away and swears under his breath. The attendant responds instantaneously. He is annoyed, and his annoyance is heightened by the fact that there is a small audience of swimmers in the changing-room. He feels disrespected and so he shouts rudely and unhelpfully across the room: 'It's not my problem mate!' He then abuses the young man by repeating that it is his own stupid fault that the money is stuck. He shouts this across the room and gets the last word. **Getting the last word is critical to macho culture.** To be fair to the attendant, what he said was not out-and-out verbal abuse but it was hardly professional behaviour. He was meant to be in charge of the changing-room and this behaviour was a response to a problem being experienced by a client there. Neither side could express what they wanted to happen clearly. They could not say how they felt. Instead they each picked up on the other's aggression and reinforced it with their own. Both wanted to get the last word with a bigger and better display of anger.

On this occasion, both weighed up the boundaries of the confrontation within the rules of macho ethics. So the bigger and older man got the last word in terms of his anger flourish; the smaller and younger teenager snarled but considered he had made his point. They kept within macho boundaries.

In another situation, in a less clear-cut situation, the whole incident could have escalated to serious verbal abuse and violence. The culture we live in encourages and condones the men's behaviour up to the point we witnessed. A dangerous situation of mutual verbal aggression had been created, which could have spiralled out of control.

Rage in a car

Road rage is a common example of macho culture. The passenger of one car and the driver of the other have their windows down and are pointing and bellowing at each other. It looks an absurd scene from the outside. Who can shout the loudest and the longest? Nobody is listening to a word that the other is saying so there is no opportunity to solve the problem. The idea of apologising for the part of the recent road manoeuvre is unthinkable. What is important is to win the display of rage and then drive off. But sometimes people in this situation forget the driving off part and step over the macho guidelines, flipping into a serious assault. Are the protagonists in this situation genuinely angry? Sometimes they are really worked up; on other occasions they have huffed and puffed their anger up to more extreme proportions than they really feel so that the macho posture can be just that little bit more vivid.

Both situations can be transferred into the school situation – the confrontation in a classroom, corridor or playground. Schools have their own specific sets of rules.

MACHO BEHAVIOUR ESCALATING A SCHOOL SITUATION

I have just watched a typical Friday lunchtime in a mixed London comprehensive school. Most of the time the behaviour and motivation of the vast majority of the pupils are good and they co-operate well with their teachers. But the lunchtime begins in a restless way, with lots of physical contact as the pupils throng down the stairs, including pushing, back slapping, mock punching and a few heads in arm-locks. It is boy on boy and boy on girl to start with, but as it spreads through the community of pupils, girls start to retaliate in kind.

About 90 per cent of the action is relatively good humoured to start with, but as the amount of physical interference builds up, it gets more and more aggressive, wild and less jokey. As lunchtime progresses, there are incidents of pushing and shoving in the dinner queues; there is a small group of boys behind it. There is a lot of macho posturing from the ring leaders and the expectation that they will be controlled by a stern disciplinarian teacher on duty. Instead the tension and aggression levels in the group of teachers rises. They are understaffed and stretched today. They have no stern disciplinarian on duty this lunchtime. The teachers' tension and anxiety lead to mutual aggression and confrontation with groups of pupils. By the end of lunchtime, pupils are running around in a large group in the playground. They are taking each other's bags and drinks while flinging plastic bottles at each other. Most respond to teacher interventions requesting them to be more sensible but a few seem to have wound themselves up in a very high state of excitement. Afternoon school starts with a real fight and two major confrontations between teachers and pupils who won't stop play-fighting to leave the playground. They are trying to settle scores with pupils who have done something to them.

This behaviour has escalated as lunchtime passed, from small beginnings into a highly unstable situation. The teachers who dealt with it were not able to intervene with decisive presence early on and stop the cycle of tension developing. As they began to feel anxious and intimidated, their interventions became more desperate, bullying and aggressive. The pupils expected them to blast their way through the problems and were not impressed by their methods of quelling them. The teachers were unable to put on a theatrical physical display of domination convincingly and the pupils weren't going to allow them any alternative strategy. They expected like to respond with like. The situation of anger escalated in teachers and pupils. The expectations of both sides on how the situation should be solved made it very difficult for there to be a successful solution to the problem.

The same pattern can be repeated at break time or at lesson change. The physical contact and interference with other pupils' body space begins. Physical aggression is often combined with cussing and insulting, which leads to a rise in temperature between the pupils, often making some very agitated and restless. They cannot settle properly in the room in which they find themselves having a lesson. In some cases they bring into the lesson inflamed squabbles which then break out at a later moment.

Some might argue that they are letting off steam after the concentration required of them within a lesson. Many try to argue that it is harmless horse-play and quite natural to all youngsters who are growing up. But I think it is more accurate to say that this kind of behaviour is likely to lead to increased tension and anger between members of the peer group. This kind of exchange leads to a build-up rather than a release of tension.

KEY INGREDIENTS FOR PURE MACHO

Male identity can be defined under the guidelines on pp. 27–30. I believe that it is this male stereotype which is the catalyst for so much verbal and physical aggression in so many school situations. There are much more exhaustive studies of boys' behaviour in the school setting. *Boys Don't Cry* by Sue Askew and Carol Ross is still an excellent book, written about schooling in the 1980s. It surveyed the tensions and anger created around the mainstream definitions of male identity, in particular, sections like 'Boys learning to be aggressive' and 'Pressures to become male'. Also a book which looks in great detail at issues around male and female gender images in the classroom is Becky Francis's *Boys, Girls and Achievement: Addressing Classroom Issues* (published by RoutledgeFalmer). The third chapter on gendered classroom culture is especially interesting in the way that transcripts of classroom conversation are used. Utterly biting and uncensored, they reveal the coercive power of aggressive 'macho' behaviour in daily interactions between pupils.

The culture of shaming

This is the most important defining characteristic of macho. It is from this that many other distinguishing characteristics link. From a very young age, little boys learn how to communicate with each other by scorning and disparagement. They learn the importance of shaming other individuals and how to stiffen their bodies to internalise the painful feelings that being on the receiving end of being shamed gives them.

Physicality: celebration of domination

Being macho involves a heightened awareness of size and the ability to dominate physically. There is a wish to test this out through show and display of oneself, and a belief that it is acceptable to infringe upon another person's body space. Macho means domineering body language such as pointing, poking or pushing and using size and strength as a way of bullying others into compliance with what you want. Physicality leads to the glorification of action and domination of others along with the disparagement of thought, feeling and reflection as ways of dealing with life.

Not showing emotion

Being a tough and hard person, emotions must be repressed, particularly ones that are regarded as soft or feminine, such as sadness, disappointment and fear. Instead conversation is about sports and sex (in the sense of physical arousal rather than emotional commitment). Any mention of relationships and personal feelings is done in a jokey way. Narrative around these issues is dealt with in terms of swapping anecdotes and having a laugh about them. The 'I feel' aspect always stays out of these stories. Fact and not feelings forms the basis for these information exchanges. There are likely to be far more exchanges about sport than about personal issues. Sport is safe ground for opinions about winning, action and mental and physical prowess.

Never admitting to a personal emotion

Owning up to the fact that you feel emotions such as sadness, disappointment or fear would be like admitting to a disease. If anybody or anything makes you feel any of these, you cover it up with abuse and the threat of violence.

Glorifying violence and verbal abuse

At one level violence is the way to solve problems. It is the only real way to preserve one's honour and self-respect. Ultimately it is necessary to win and this can be done only by shouting louder than your rival or by physical intervention to shut them up. The use of violence is linked to success. A problem can be solved not by expressing one clear personal feeling but by showing rage (a whole jumble of unfocused emotions). At another level, violence and verbal abuse can be entertaining to watch and talk about.

Going forward, never backward

In situations of conflict you must stand your ground physically. You must have the last word. The more unfair the odds against you, the braver and more glorious the individual is who does not budge.

Never apologising

Admitting you have made a mistake is totally unacceptable. Apology is a sign of weakness.

Using bad language with reference to female anatomy

Some of the most treasured insults or cusses are ones which identify another man as being soft or vulnerable like a woman.

Obsessive hatred of homosexuality

The worst put-down you can give another male is to accuse him of being gay or a 'batty'.

Sexism

Macho involves very sexist attitudes to the way that girls should look, the views they should have and the way they should behave, emphasising the woman as a sex object for male gratification.

Fanatical defence of mother as the most precious human relationship

To cuss another boy's mother is the ultimate insult. Many of the worst put-downs will involve explicit reference to sexual relations with another male's mother. This one cuss starts more fights than anything else!

Value system based on revenge

This is very much the Old Testament philosophy of 'eye for an eye' and 'tooth for a tooth'. Retaliation for what has been done to you and yours forms an essential part of the culture.

Respect

Respect is a term of brotherhood bonding rather than an empathy, enthusiasm and interest in another personality. It includes respect from one male for another male's physical prowess, respect for another male's ability to fight and respect for the daring exploits of another man. It does not mean respecting another person's individual rights, feelings and points of view. It is respect for physical presence. Bonding between individuals can take place if one proves loyalty by fighting others.

Violence as entertainment

Violence and verbal abuse provide an adrenalin flow. They are exciting. Listen to adolescent boys anecdotalise, talking about the size of guns, firing them, how fast they are and how big they are, or how Mike Tyson the boxer punched somebody to pulp.

Status

Those involved in macho behaviour often gain a lot of status from it. They are good fighters. It has given them respect (as defined above) and it gives them power and influence over others. It makes them feel important. They have a lot to gain by perpetuating it.

REFINED MACHO: THE NORMAL DAILY BOUNDARIES IN SCHOOL

Most pupils accept limitation to the pure macho culture out of common sense and their own self-preservation. In the same way as the two males who argued in the swimming pool changing-room or in their cars usually stick to invisible rules, most school pupils know the boundaries of their own abusive banter. They appreciate that you have to back off when someone is bigger than you, can shout louder or has the power to get you kicked out of class or school. They accept that if people keep on abusing each other in class, the disorder it creates will stop a teacher from giving them a proper lesson.

Unfortunately the bottom quarter of the pupil population in many schools are already so bored with what the teachers are trying to teach that the rules of refined macho count for much less with them. They will push, poke and jostle in the corridor but they don't stop when they come into the classroom. They will go on larking about and posturing so that it has a serious effect on the lesson. A minority of these pupils will recognise no boundaries at any level. Once they start getting wound up with the macho bravado, they find it very difficult to back off. These are the pupils who have unhealthy anger problems. They may well know the unwritten rules of macho but once they get sucked into the process they can get so provoked as to lose it completely.

What is clear is that macho culture regularly unsettles good relationships – and good learning situations – in a school. It encourages instability. When blended with situations where many pupils are low skilled in literacy and numeracy and poorly motivated towards the curriculum, a disruptive cocktail comes into play.

TOMBOY MACHO

Macho behaviour is predominantly a boy onto boy and boy onto girl problem. But girls can get bad bouts of it too. Physical and verbal abuse becomes an important part of their identity. They are happy to bully others using their physicality to dominate them. Like their male counterparts they get hooked into the macho styles of behaviour. And they find it very hard to show their underlying vulnerable feelings or express them in a direct and assertive way. Clearly some girls adopt this kind of behaviour as a form of self-defence against the aggression and the abuse they receive from the boys around them. They fight like with like. They may feel this is necessary in school and in their out-of-school relations with the opposite sex.

But a major influence on girls aping boys' macho behaviour is the 'warrior babe' image encouraged by the pop music girl bands and girls' magazines. A warrior babe is tough and independent. According to the mythology, she can fight, swear and drink as much as any boy. She can pick up her men for physical gratification and drop them. She can kick and punch her way through a row with another girl or boy. She is the embodiment of the macho culture we have looked at that glorifies physicality, revenge, verbal abuse and violence. If a girl is a 'warrior babe', she cannot fall victim to that hurtful, sexist, macho slur of being labelled a 'slapper' or a 'slag'.

Chapter 5

Where does the macho culture come from?

Macho culture is a controversial and complex area. It is not my intention in this book to do a complex analysis of it. But it is important to demonstrate that teenage girls and boys are bombarded with information and images that both encourage and reinforce macho-style behaviour. It is hardly surprising they import it into one of their most important social settings – their relationships in school.

SOCIALISATION AND SEXUAL STEREOTYPING

Macho behaviour has an historical evolution which can be described simply. Traditionally men have been seen as the breadwinners, doing hard physical labour. Women's jobs were to stay in the home and service the men's needs as well as nurture the children. From the earliest of ages the male is encouraged to see himself in terms of action and physicality, the female in terms of emotion.

At the very beginning of life the boy/girl socialisation process begins. It can start with colour coding in the first few days – boys with blue and girls with pink. Then the boys are given the soldiers and other action games while the girls get the dolls and teddies to look after. It isn't long before the relatives begin to describe the young boy children as looking big and strong and the girls as pretty and sweet. The fathers start to engage in much more rough and tumble play with their sons. They encourage them into physical action and sport. Girls are reminded to sit with their legs together. At this stage even the right-on parents who are aware of sexual stereotyping and wish to challenge it find it very hard to stop their boys wanting certain kinds of toys and playing in a certain way. The influences of gender regimentation are too strong to be resisted successfully in just the family. From the moment that children get up in the morning and switch on the television they are bombarded with advertising that incessantly sets the boundaries of sexual stereotyping. As the pre-teen years turn to the teenage ones, the sexual stereotyping comes into a new phase of rigid definition. Boys must be brave, strong and action based (not much change from before). But not being little any more means that the scope to show a wider range of more vulnerable or sensitive emotions is even more severely frowned upon. Boys are tightly laced into their role model strait-jacket which encourages them to explore aspects of the destructive macho behaviour with a renewed vigour.

Like all things in life, new behaviours are possible and there are many significant deviations from the system of rigid gender stereotyping I have described. But it would be foolish to pretend that most girls and boys are not heavily influenced by simple gender archetypes in their teenage years of schooling.

MACHO, SOCIAL CLASS AND COMMUNITY VALUES

Macho behaviour seems to feature in all social classes and in most cultural and ethnic backgrounds. The strongest influence on the aggressive laddish behaviour seems to come from the father as a role model. I have lost count of the number of times that I have heard a male parent say that he has told his son to stand up for himself and hit anybody who shows him disrespect. Or the times I have heard families threaten physical violence on another pupil or their family because of a dispute that starts out of school. This anger is very strong in the value system of certain communities. To defend you must attack. An argument is settled by shouting longest and loudest. Winning is done physically and fear must be instilled into your opponent. They have to be taught to show respect and this respect is won physically and not mentally. To deny it completely would be unrealistic. But to place such heavy emphasis on it on all occasions undermines the other constructive ways that people can communicate with each other.

MACHO IMAGES EVERYWHERE

The English football match is typical. Players verbally and physically abuse each other on the pitch and the fans brawl off it. Despite decrying football hooliganism, there is a fascination in the media for the gang rivalry off the pitch and the players' power struggles on it. Similarly, wrestling and boxing are mass media sports in which size, aggression and violence are glorified.

Hollywood has aggression and violence at the core of many of its storylines. There are whole genres of film with the super macho hero. There are hundreds of film narratives where heroes assert their moral integrity by fighting violence with violence, abuse with abuse. The goodie wins by beating up and killing the baddie in a superior demonstration of machismo. The audience is taken along with this scenario – we are willing the goodie to teach the baddie a lesson and get revenge.

Even the simplest children's television programme about two under-11 football teams has the coaches arguing. The scene climaxes when the good one punches the bad one on the nose and breaks it. No comment is made on the physical assault. It shuts the other man up so it is portrayed as morally right.

What are boys and girls supposed to make of all the constant glorification of physical powers, aggression and violence (the emotional consequences of which are never shown)? What are they supposed to make of the constant use of violence for entertainment? What are they supposed to make of the paucity of emotional expression from the male role models surrounding them, other than endless demonstrations of puffed-up aggression or blind rage?

CASE STUDY

Take the example of one pupil, Billy, who was referred to me for anger management, having been involved in a number of fights and incidents of physical intimidation of other pupils.

Billy's first session was fascinating for the way it illustrated the archetypal macho lad:

1 You have to fight to defend your honour.
2 Violence is entertaining. It provides excitement. It is a celebration of physical strength.
3 Violence gives Billy status. He is good at fighting.
4 The consequences of the action are thought about only in terms of who wins. So if Billy were to lose or get hurt, then it would become a matter for the wider family and cousins. Getting retribution or revenge was far higher on the agenda in terms of respect than the possible school-based consequences of being permanently excluded or getting in trouble with the police.
5 Billy acknowledged having an uncontrollable temper when aroused, but he admitted to this as if it were a kind of boast.
6 The only emotion Billy was prepared to admit to was loving his Mum. This was given as a reason why he would never hit her.
7 I probed him about the time when he attacked his best friend, which had happened after Billy had slipped while climbing on a wall and hurt his leg. Finally he admitted to one other emotion. He said he had wanted his friend to ask him if he was hurt or not, and he didn't. He had been very disappointed that no enquiries were made about his welfare. So he became physically violent rather than show his feelings.

If you look back at my original list on super-macho (see pp. 27–30) you will find that Billy fits in with many of its key points – almost line by line. His attitudes are typical of many pupils who have been referred to me for anger management.

THE FINE LINE BETWEEN MACHO BEHAVIOUR AND DECISIVE PRESENCE IN SCHOOLS

There is a fine line between having presence and personality which you use to make a decisive intervention with confidence, and bullying that uses size, presence and character in an aggressive way. Perhaps the problem is that most teachers find it very difficult to do either successfully. Only a very few people in the teaching profession can intervene successfully with their charismatic personality. A few more can bully people into submission by physical intimidation or by relentless punishment. But the vast majority of teachers fail spectacularly at both.

Yet there is a huge emphasis on these styles of discipline; they carry very high status. Few teachers do it effectively while many try to copy it with ungainly and often disastrous results. It is the dominant kind of discipline mechanism in some schools, and pupils expect to be imposed upon and dominated by a strong, sometimes aggressive adult.

But what happens if you are part of the majority who just can't do it like that? If teachers cannot overpower a difficult situation with a powerful character display of energy and physical domination, they can often get boxed into a corner. Tricky situations include a group of youngsters posturing, jostling and cussing each other in the corridor, a classroom where there is a lot of high-energy restless behaviour or when many of the pupils are poorly motivated and have low academic skills. They are bored and seek entertainment but the teacher cannot provide them with a convincing display of macho behaviour to conquer their misbehaviour.

The majority of teachers have a daily fear of failure of this situation. They feel uncomfortable and intimidated when faced with macho behaviour from individual pupils or groups of youngsters and they try to assert themselves in a traditional person-dominating way. It is what teachers expect other teachers to do. It is what pupils expect from their teachers. But trying to show pupils you are the boss makes many adults in schools feel tense, insecure and defensive as they attempt to do it. Their body language tells the real story despite the amount of shouting and aggressive posturing they display. They would be fine if they could appeal to the pupils' motivation to learn, using their own subject knowledge and desire to communicate it. But they are stumped when dealing with a bored, physically restless class who are already ill at ease and frustrated with being stuck behind a desk lesson after lesson.

The net result is that teachers get very angry and their insecurity leads to confusion. In such circumstances they fail to set clear parameters of expectations to the pupils. Many other people get very angry with each other and the teacher. The key ingredient for a successful lesson – the establishment of good supportive relationships in the room – fails to happen. Lesson momentum cannot build from such weak foundations. It is the perfect breeding ground for incidents of unhealthy anger.

ENTERTAINMENT, TELLING OFF AND PUNISHMENT

I have previously mentioned the entertainment factor of the teacher giving a telling off, but what does this mean exactly? To explain it I need to refer you to a typical classroom scenario. A few pupils have started to drift off task. They have stopped reading the text you are trying to go through with them and have started to kick each other under the table and talk among themselves. You use the technique of extinction and blank this low-level interruption by trying to encourage pupils back to their reading task. You give a key miscreant a couple of stony-faced glares, but you don't want to lose the momentum of the reading by confronting this pupil and getting into an energy-sapping answering-back session. Then a strange phenomenon kicks into action. Pupils start exhorting you to punish them. They ask why you are not shouting or giving out detentions to the people who are misbehaving. They chastise you for not being strict.

Ask yourself the question: would they do this in a lesson with a stern disciplinarian who controls the class with his or her dominating presence? The answer of course is 'no'. This is because the vast majority of the pupils are fascinated and fearful of being at the receiving end of a dressing down in this situation. They certainly would not want to draw attention to themselves by asking for members of the group to be punished. But they know that at some point in the lesson the teacher will entertain everybody with either a mild or a strong outburst of asserting ego over some hapless individual.

When they implore a teacher to punish the group or people in the group, they are hoping to draw them into a confrontational scenario through which they can watch them flounder and then lose. They want the sport of seeing their teacher shout and make threats which they won't or can't keep. They want to see an answering-back session in which the pupil gets the better of the teacher. In the confusion that such situations produce, there is cover for other forms of pupil interaction and general mucking about. And if the teacher wins a confrontation with a pupil and bucks the trend, then that is also entertaining to watch.

It is vital to understand that for many pupils it is the human interaction pupil to pupil and pupil to teacher which stimulates them more than the curriculum.

NON-MACHO DRESSING DOWNS

In the current world of schools you will not always find it easy to avoid the macho style of discipline because the pupils' verbal and physical abuse of each other and of you is very real. The behaviours described in the survey at the beginning of this book are going to challenge you every day you are in a school. There are still going to be many times when you could get sucked into confrontation. Later in this book I shall outline the various strategies you can use to deal with a pupil who is very angry. I will suggest ways in which a school can handle problems of abuse and aggression a whole lot better through institutional teamwork. But for the moment I simply suggest some things to remember if you want to avoid failing to dominate the pupils with a show of macho posturing.

Giving a telling off, without making a fool of yourself

1 Recognise the situations where a stern response may be expected from pupils and other teachers around you. (See the original lists for in and out of classroom situations on pp. 5–7.) Be aware of your body tensing and your feelings of panic, frustration and inadequacy. Don't roll up your sleeves and jump into a barney. Make a conscious effort not to do so.

2 Try to pick off individuals who are challenging your authority. If possible, separate them (although you should ensure that you are never alone with a pupil) from the audience that they will be anxious to impress. Give them their instructions in isolation, in a low voice which others cannot hear.

3 Use your knowledge of the group. Go for the most compliant individual, who is most likely to do as he or she is asked. One obedient person can start the others doing what you asked for.

4 Back off a bit when you have made a request and give people time and space to follow your instructions. If you stand over them, they may feel there is too much loss of face in following your commands.

5 Go for anybody you know in the group, if most of them are unknown pupils.

6 Don't start aping macho body language and tone of voice, especially if you are in some way trying to copy other teachers' styles. Be yourself.

7 Be prepared to repeat an instruction calmly but purposefully. If you are being ignored or shouted at, just keep doing what you are doing. Don't panic or it will sound in your voice.

8 If possible try to use humour to coax and cajole pupils along. If they respond positively in any way, it will help your body to relax.

9 Warn the pupils that you know that failure to follow your instructions will result in consequences later. It is probably best not to specify what they are as you could be setting yourself up for actions you will find difficult to take.

10 Avoid shouting, pointing and attempting to dominate. It is a high-risk strategy in a confrontation because you may lose.

11 Remember that pupils will be reading your body language rather than listening closely to what you say. If you are unconvincingly macho, your body language will be hunched, tight, crumpled and thus you are defeated in some way before you start to assert yourself.

12 If you know you are going to follow up a pupil, you can let them disobey you, ignore you or simply storm off. You keep your dignity in front of other pupils by avoiding escalating a confrontation and losing it.

13 Always follow up pupils. Pick them up later that day or the next.

14 Have a clear idea of how you will take them to task about what they did earlier and of what you will say to gain the moral, intellectual and emotional high ground.

15 Get reinforcements from another colleague if you are worried that the pupil may continue to be insolent and

abusive to you. It is good for pupils to see that their teachers work as a team.

16 Make your interventions when you are ready and prepared. But don't forget to make them. If you don't follow through, you won't begin the process of establishing yourself.

17 Remember that even if you felt powerless and humiliated in the situation where macho behaviour was called upon and not supplied by you, it is infinitely better to sort things out later in a more sensible way than get into a confrontation which you lose.

MACHO AND THE RESTRICTION OF GENDER ROLES

'I didn't say you had a moustache, I said you were a whore.'

This comment was made by a Year 9 boy to a new female teacher in a boys' school. She was subjected to a protracted campaign of vicious sexual abuse when she arrived at this inner-city school. The moustache comment referred to the fact that she had a couple of visible strands of facial hair above her lip. The boy who made the remark had been at pains to justify himself by saying that he had not in fact made a comment about this facial hair. His insult had been no part of the class's ongoing verbal abuse about the teacher's upper lip. His description of her as a 'whore' was different and as it was a new line of abuse it was not as serious as him contributing to the initial line of persecution the class was pursuing. This bizarre justification for appalling rudeness reflects just how ingrained sexist abuse is for boys. Facial hair or any other deviation from the young male fantasy of how a desirable female should look will lead to relentless comment and mockery. Too fat, too thin, beard, moustache, hair under the arms – the list is endless.

Male role models

In boys' schools male role models are rigidly defined. Men who in any way demonstrate behaviour different from straight-backed, repressed-emotion macho are seen as dangerous deviants. They are likely to be branded as gay. Men who are the most readily accepted are those acting out the role of macho lad. As fully fledged adults they are bigger and more imposing than the teenage boys. They can command the respect of the lads. They are louder and more powerful than the aspiring Year 11 lads. They are the leaders of the gang, even though they are supposed to have crossed the professional divide that separates student and teacher.

In mixed schools the role of macho group leader is diluted by the presence of girls. Here the male role models are allowed broader scope. Male teachers with effeminate traits cannot be branded as homosexual because the female members of the class relate to them – perhaps flirt with them and vice versa. This causes confusion in the minds of the boys but they cannot ignore the girls' natural reaction. They are unhappy with another male as competition for the girls' attention, even if he is a teacher. Non-macho male teachers who attract the girls will be admired, envied and loathed simultaneously. They will often get significant amounts of anger and aggression directed towards them from the boys. The very fact that they are prepared to show any kind of sexuality in the way they express themselves is seen as seditious by the males. It makes many of them feel very uncomfortable.

Women teachers

Women teachers will come in for the most vile abuse, particularly in boys' schools where gender stereotypes are the most rigid. Some of the worst abuse is reserved for women who the boys find sexually attractive. It can be that the more they fancy her, the more they denigrate her. But women who they don't fancy will get picked on whatever their age if they show any vulnerable feelings. The boys seem comfortable with a female teacher only when they can pigeon hole her into another safe stereotype such as 'mother' or 'bossy auntie'.

In the mixed environment, this attitude towards women is softened and the extreme macho tendencies of the boys are tempered towards female staff by the presence of girls. The non-macho male role model can also gain acceptance quicker. But girls can also police women teachers, commenting on their personal appearance and dress sense.

The stronger the desire of the pupils to use the knowledge and expertise the teacher has to offer, the quicker a determined teacher can overcome the problems of verbal abuse by showing that their teaching skills are more important than gender stereotypes. But where classes have large numbers of pupils who are poorly skilled and disinterested in the academic curriculum, the lure of an interesting lesson is less of an appeal, and the promise of abusing the teacher offers more entertainment.

Clearly the rigid role model stereotypes that adolescent boys and girls set up for themselves and their teachers lead to a lot of repression. Repression is a natural breeding ground for bullying, abuse and violence. **Repression encourages anger to build up because it discourages people from communicating honestly with each other**. It stops people being themselves. Yet role demarcation in schools and the suppression of some identities with the glorification of others regularly create such situations.

HOW DO SCHOOLS DEAL WITH THE VERBAL ABUSE OF TEACHERS?

Some schools do very well to combat verbal abuse aimed at teachers, while others are less assured. Some teachers may be advised to ignore the problem.

Often those in a position of power may be individuals who have risen through the system because of their forceful management style. They are underlyingly contemptuous of teachers who whinge about this kind of rudeness from pupils. They often make token gestures at solving the problems, trying to bully pupils out of doing it rather than having an effective whole school policy for challenging sexism and educating a change in pupil behaviour. They describe establishing an effective relationship with a class in very macho terms as similar to coming through a trial by ordeal. They see an effective teacher as one who breaks the class's spirit of rebellion and establishes obedience through the force of their will. Those that come through are those who are prepared to stand their ground in very challenging circumstances.

If a headteacher tells the staff to ignore provocation and make light of it, they will soon shut up. They may already be feeling embarrassed and undermined by the pupils' bullying. They will simply stop mentioning the problems they are having. By turning a blind eye to these problems or by making half-hearted interventions, schools end up reinforcing them. **Macho behaviour continues to damage staff teamwork, teacher–pupil relations and pupil–pupil relationships.**

Part 2

Whole school and classroom strategies for dealing with anger

Chapter 6

The anger cycle

Pupils who become angry are giving an emotional reaction to needs they perceive themselves to have, which are not being met. Anger can also be used as a manipulative strategy by a pupil to get what they want. It can be used to bully and intimidate.

HEALTHY ANGER

'Healthy anger' can get things done and solve problems for an individual. It will rise when an important feeling needs to be expressed and will disappear when that expression has taken place. There is a sense of good timing to healthy anger. It is used for the right length of time, on specific occasions and with appropriate people.

When anger is expressed this way, it provides an opportunity for resolving a situation. It is a positive act to solve a problem. Even when expressed strongly it does not denigrate the other person and their point of view. Thus, if a person is angry with you in a healthy way they will make a point forcefully and really get to the nub of the matter. It is a clean surge of energy. You might feel knocked back by the force involved in the intensity of their anger, but despite your shock, they manage to convey very directly what their problem is and you understand it, without feeling violated and abused. Their anger does not put you down in any way, but it brings you up sharply.

UNHEALTHY ANGER OR RAGE

Anger which comes out in an unhealthy way damages relationships. It is aggressive, destructive and leaves others feeling violated and abused. Unhealthy anger will involve verbal abuse and often lead to physical aggression. It is better described as rage.

Rage is a whole mix of explosive and unfocused emotions. It often turns into an extended violent outburst or tirade. In the onslaught the other person is often personally attacked on a whole range of fronts rather than the person saying what the specific thing is that they themselves are feeling angry about. 'What you said to her just now made me feel really terrible' might be rephrased into an unhealthy rant as 'You always let me down: you are a completely useless idiot!'

Rage offers the illusion of a strong resolution to a problem for the people who suffer it. It is often described by them as like scratching an itch. Having a rant does provide a short-term release of tension. It may give an immediate feeling of power as the rage bullies other parties into doing what has been demanded or at least cowes them into silence. Frightened people give in to the wishes of the angry person. In the long term, however, verbally and physically abusive anger introduces insecurity into relationships. Bullying destroys trust and makes any future resolution of problems much more difficult. The physical effect of getting into an uncontrollable rage leaves the protagonist feeling depressed and low, when they have burned themselves out. (See Stage Five of the anger cycle later in this chapter, pp. 55–6.)

A teacher who has been repeatedly abused in class by a pupil will often be tense and fearful of a repeat performance. This will make it harder and harder for there to be a constructive relationship between the two of them. The same applies the other way round if a teacher rages at a pupil.

PROBLEMS FOR RAGERS IN SCHOOL

1 Ragers are feared and detested by teachers for their potential to destroy a lesson.
2 They bewilder and irritate other pupils because a 'funny turn' from one of them can destroy a lesson. Pupils like a laugh and joke but these ragers take it too far.
3 Angry pupils get caught up in their own emotional agenda. This often blocks them from giving their full attention to the learning process. They are much more likely to fall behind.
4 If they fall behind the experience of frustration and failure is likely to reinforce their emotional volatility.
5 They are disliked by teachers, pupils and by the parents of the pupils. If their uncontrolled outbursts threaten the security of others, they find themselves excluded swiftly and permanently. They will have few defenders.

PROBLEMS FOR RAGERS OUT OF SCHOOL

1 Angry teenagers usually turn into angry adults. Their temper outbursts are more likely to lead them into trouble with the law, particularly crimes such as physical assault, criminal damage and domestic violence.
2 Alternative educational provision for them is often scarce and very expensive. It is likely to become even more rare in the future as the current policy of social inclusion reduces placements out of the mainstream. But alternative provision, even if it were available, does not give pupils the chance to gain access to as wide a curriculum as other pupils.
3 Pupils who have a lot of anger are likely to have low self-esteem. If they are finding it difficult to value themselves, they will find it harder still to value the other people around them. Building and sustaining meaningful relationships in their later life will be very tough.

WHAT CAN A SCHOOL DO TO MINIMISE THE CHANCE OF UNCONTROLLED OUTBURSTS?

Theoretically, schools may be one of the most stable environments in which some angry young people spend time. They should be good places for working on curing their anger. Often, however, this is not the case in practice; schools are even less likely to tolerate individuals with the tendency for anger than their own families.

Schools are large communities and they believe it is possible to control large numbers of individuals only through exacting sets of rules. They are places of formality and systems. They are places in which ethos is controlled by an extended hierarchy of teachers, middle managers and senior teams. This makes them a lot more inflexible than a family unit where a child with a predisposition for rage is more easily absorbed.

Non-conformity in behaviour sticks out a mile in a big institution with lots of rules. Individuals who don't conform find themselves squeezed by the system. They are regarded as a severe threat because many teachers believe that if one pupil is seen to get away with unacceptable behaviour, then this will have a ricochet effect on all the other borderline malcontents who are just waiting for a lead to misbehave.

We shall examine good strategies for dealing with angry behaviours in Part 3 of this book, but it is important to stress at this stage that the anger will be better managed in schools where there is a comprehensive approach to behaviour management across the board. An approach including a whole school behaviour policy which challenges macho behaviour in all its forms and recognises that anger management is something that all its pupils need to be taught explicitly. Again, we shall return to these issues in Chapters 8, 9 and 10.

THE ANGER CYCLE

When a pupil becomes uncontrollably angry, it is helpful if the teacher understands the cycle of anger. It is sound advice in and out of the classroom and will make it less likely that an aggressive incident will lead to gross verbal abuse or a physical attack on another pupil or the teacher.

The anger cycle can be described as running in five stages.

- **Stage One: agitation and early warning signs**. At this stage the person is beginning to warm up but he or she can probably be calmed down again with the correct handling and an attempt to solve the problem in a constructive way.
- **Stage Two: escalation**. Physiological arousal is getting greater by the minute. The heating-up process is well under way. Intervention can still take place but it will be harder to make it successful with every second that goes by.
- **Stage Three: crisis**. The spark catches the gunpowder and there is an explosion. During the giving off of heat, no rational communication with the angry person is possible. At this stage the danger of violence is at its highest.
- **Stage Four: peaking and recovery**. The cooling-down process can begin as the outburst of energy is over. This is a volatile and unstable stage as the wrong response from the teacher could lead to a rapid reheat.
- **Stage Five: post crisis, depression and negativity**. The rage has burned up an incredible amount of the body's energy and the person is left feeling flat, negative and depressed. It is only at this stage that the angry pupil may be able to listen to a rational appraisal of what has happened. It is only now that the angry person may be calm enough to express the feelings that took them into their earlier rage in a sensible way.

THE ANGER CYCLE IN DETAIL

Stage One: agitation and early warning signs

The problem begins when something happens to agitate the thoughts and feelings of a person who is capable of vengeful rage. The incident or action by others will be interpreted by them as a major threat to their self-esteem and self-image. The incident will set alight a fuse that connects to the gunpowder barrel. While the fuse is lit, there is still time to intervene in a way that will stop the anger spiralling out of control.

Stage Two: escalation

As the conflict works itself up inside the pupil, the body will respond to adrenalin. The early warning signs of a rage coming on usually show themselves at this point. The mouth goes dry, body muscles tense and breathing becomes shallow as blood pressure rises. It is often a characteristic at this point for a person to think the same injured thought repeatedly or to mutter or talk to themselves during the time that their temperature rises. The longer the escalation period lasts physically and mentally, the less likely the person will be able to respond to rational solutions.

Stage Three: crisis

The fuse runs out and the flame catches the gunpowder. An explosion occurs. Later in the book I describe the crisis in terms of the phrase 'the moment of fatal peril'. Sometimes a twinge, shiver spasm or unbearable itch converts arousal into blind rage. One of my pupils described it vividly as 'popping'. But the words 'blind rage' are very apt, as the person who has it is blind to all but their own expression of anger. They are not capable of listening or understanding what is being said to them by others. They may well put themselves and others in a situation of danger.

An interesting documentary on the life of professional door-keepers (bouncers) in the night-clubs of a West Country city came up with some apt thoughts on the subject. The doorkeepers always try to intervene before Stage Three erupts because experience has taught them that when people lose their tempers, it is usually impossible to pull the situation back and solve it rationally. The organisation's key aim for the safety of its own members and the general public is to nip problems in the bud, by going in at Stage One of a confrontation, when the anger cycle is just heating up. In fact, the earlier the better.

Stage Four: peaking and recovery

A cooling and calming process may now set in, but it is very volatile and unstable. In this period the anger begins to subside but it would be easy to rekindle it, by intervening inappropriately in the problem. The body is still on alert and prepared for action. The feelings inside the person are still confused and vulnerable. It would not take much to revert into another angry outburst. It is often at this stage that the school hierarchy attempt a clumsy disciplinarian intervention.

Stage Five: post crisis, depression and negativity

The crisis stage of rage is very tiring. Such a high state of mental and physical arousal leaves the body exhausted. With the onset of tiredness comes the ability to listen and think clearly again. The pupil begins to feel unhappy and anxious about what has just happened. They often feel guilty about the incident. They will be fearful of the consequences of their actions, which previously they had brushed aside as they worked themselves up into a rage.

Guilt blended with remorse gives a positive chance for the individual to apologise, make amends and build positive bridges for the future.

The anger cycle can still be reignited during this recovery phase. It will often take two hours or more for a teenager to calm down after a serious outburst of rage. If the protagonists involved in a serious dispute find themselves in close proximity to each other, then they could easily spark each other off into the anger cycle again.

Schools are busy places but it is better to wait and let pupils involved in a violent situation calm down for *at the very least* forty-five minutes before trying to unpick the incident in which they were involved.

Chapter 7

How can a teacher intervene in the anger cycle?

Get in at Stage One or early Stage Two in the anger cycle (see p. 54). Recognise the early warning signals:

- the voice being raised
- agitated body movement
- interference in somebody else's body space
- physical repetitive movements such as pacing up and down
- muttering and swinging on a chair
- screwing up a piece of paper or scribbling on an exercise book
- changes in facial expression such as frowning or sorry looking eyes
- changes in eye contact, either to excessive eye balling or making no contact at all
- sudden change in body language or posture
- signs of rapid mood swing.

Look in the invisible mirror at yourself. What you are looking for in the pupil, you should be checking for in yourself. If you are gearing up for an expected confrontation with a person, you will be tensing up and beginning to exhibit many of the above traits yourself. You will be setting yourself on collision course with your mirror image.

HOW CAN YOU INTERVENE SUCCESSFULLY?

Each individual situation is different:

- Each situation has to be judged as a one off.
- Every person involved in it has to be regarded as an individual.

The better you know the pupil, the more you will be able to tell how physiologically aroused they are. The better you know yourself, the more you will be able to assess how angry you are getting.

At this stage you have two choices: extinction or intervention.

- **Extinction**: ignore the problem and hope it will sort itself out. Concentrate on keeping your teaching momentum.
- **Intervention**: jump in with all guns blazing and dominate the persons and the situation.

Advantages and disadvantages of extinction

It could be dangerous to ignore a problem for the sake of lesson momentum as this gives the pupil's rage longer to build up. If there is going to be an aggressive outburst, pretending it is not going to happen only delays and makes it much more likely that the outburst, when it comes, will be even worse.

However, it could be a problem that will calm down or disappear if you ignore it and get on with your lesson. Would you want to get into confrontation with one pupil who shouts out if you have got the rest of the class listening to you teach? Extinction is a great way of de-escalating, providing you have got a good sense of timing about the situation and the characters involved. This comes through personal experience and by watching other skilled practitioners in classrooms.

Advantages and disadvantages of intervention

Decisive intervention and domination of a situation are the equivalent of flinging a large bucket of cold water on a small fire and putting it out. It could restore order immediately and with minimum fuss or disturbance to the lesson. A confrontation won early in the lesson will set the teacher's agenda for the rest of it.

But a failed intervention of this type is a high risk. If it is mistimed and backfires on you, the pupil's behaviour could escalate into crisis stage and full-blown rage. You could end up with a lot of egg on your face.

Strangely it is the high-risk strategy that teachers in schools prize the most. It is to this strategy that they turn to with disastrous results, time after time. But can they be blamed for choosing this preference? It is the high-risk intervention that the pupils seem to admire the most. It is this kind of intervention that, if successful, gains them the respect of other teachers. **It is the only strategy that the significant minority of macho pupil disrupters think is real discipline.**

OTHER DIFFUSING STRATEGIES OPEN TO THE CLASSROOM TEACHER

There are a number of possible strategies:

- distraction for the pupil
- distraction for the teacher
- relocation of the pupil
- relocation of the teacher
- changing the teaching materials and teaching styles
- emergency changes of pupil activity
- changing your mindset
- physical closeness
- calming body language
- using jokes and humour

- mood matching
- active listening.

Let's look at each one in turn.

Distraction for the pupil

Try to find a way of getting the pupil's attention on to something else. Get it away from what is bugging them. For example you can remind them of the positive attitude they have had up to that point in the lesson or during other lessons. Ask them a question about the work which you know they have a good answer to. Try to give them some one-to-one help on what you are reading and writing that lesson.

Distraction for the teacher

You can feel your anger and frustration rising. It is important to try to distract yourself from getting embroiled in confrontation mode. What have you already done that day at or before school which is positive? Who are the pupils in the lesson who really want to learn? Have you helped them enough? Can you find some inspiration and get the whole class to concentrate with a new dramatic explanation of the work you are doing?

Relocation of the pupil

Get the pupil away from the environment that is stressful. This is likely to stop escalation to the 'popping' point. Move them away from the pupils they are interacting poorly with. Get them outside the room. Send them on an urgent errand.

Relocation allows disengagement and a cooling off to occur. It is a vital diffusion strategy and we shall return to it later when looking at the pilot anger management course, where it is renamed Time Out (see pp. 107–10).

Relocation of the teacher

If the anger is directed at you, it is still important for either you or the pupil to disengage and relocate. This gives both parties the chance to cool down. As the teacher you can move away to another part of the room and help somebody else. You can brush aside a rude comment or a muttered remark and deal with something else. The matter can be returned to later and dealt with at a time that suits you and when the situation has become less charged. **Remember that a postponed confrontation can peter out over time into no confrontation at all.**

Changing the teaching materials and teaching styles

Certain classroom activities cause high stress to some pupils. Certain classroom activities cause high stress to some teachers. To avoid tension and anger you should try to think about how the lesson itself may be contributing to problems in the group dynamics.

1 Dense texts with heavy demands of reading and comprehension skills make pupils with shaky reading ability restless and edgy. They may seek to entertain themselves off task by interacting with other pupils. The demands of difficult independent writing may do the same thing to pupils with literacy difficulties. There is often a strong correlation between pupils with high levels of anger, low levels of concentration and general learning and literacy problems.
2 Activities which lead to a lot of unstructured movement around the room are not a good idea.
3 The golden rule is that if the task is too difficult and/or the instructions about how to do it are unclear, then the chances of getting angry aggressive incidents rise.
4 Find the learning styles that suit the pupils as much as you can. Change your teaching style if necessary, not the other way round.

5 Look for things that are going well in the lesson. Use rewards and lots of praise for positive achievement. You can often catch people doing the right thing if you are on the look out for it.

6 For more advice on producing good lesson materials you need to look at other books on the subject as there are plenty of them. My book *Surviving and Succeeding in Difficult Classrooms* may be a help (ISBN 0–415–18523–8).

Emergency changes of pupil activity

With one pupil who had destructive rages that were capable of engulfing him very quickly, I would change his activity by getting him into the playground to kick a football with me or using his learning support assistant to get him out of the room. This was possible only because there were two adults in the room at the time.

Changing your mindset

Certain situations with some pupils get into a mental deadlock. The same cycle of aggression and confrontation keeps on repeating itself. Friday period 6 with the bottom group or every Tuesday before lunch with the three surly girls that sit near the front. Often a sudden change of reaction from the teacher will wrong foot the pupils and break that vicious cycle.

At the moment you find that you always end up shouting. You get into a situation where you have ten people back in detention. You get into confrontation over the rule about mobile phones with one of those girls and she flounces out of the room. **But suppose you reacted differently?** You gave the bottom set last thing on the Friday afternoon a task they were not expecting. You ignored the mobile phone but praised the girl for doing the first part of her work well. You gave rewards to the people who worked well Friday period 6 and cancelled the detentions for any of the naughties who started to work better before the end of the lesson. In all these actions you will be breaking a chain of negativity that both you and the class expect to get sucked into. They are expecting you to scowl, and you smile. They are expecting you to yell, and you repeat your explanation for a third time in an even calmer voice.

You could be bursting the anger bubble in the room like a pin to a balloon.

Physical closeness

While some pupils will respond well to physical closeness when they are very angry, others may react in very different ways. Decisions about such approaches need to be made with great caution. When making such a decision you need to understand very clearly what the school's expectations and requirements are. A good School Policy or Code of Conduct should be based on an awareness of Teacher Union Guidelines and the Head-teacher's Handbook, in which clear advice on physical contact and closeness is given.

Calming body language

It is possible that they will respond to your body language of calming gestures. Slow, open-palm movements which press down at about chest height are effective. Football referees use them when players start to get angry about a disputed call or a bad foul. Movements which slow down as you do them, so they encourage the other person's aggressive arousal to copy you and slow down itself, are useful. Body position that is side on rather than head on in a confrontational situation helps diffuse tensions. Hands behind the back rather than being used to make points and gesticulate calm difficult situations by reducing incursions into the agitated person's body space.

Using jokes and humour

This is a very high-risk strategy that could infuse rather than defuse. If the timing is right and the humour wrong foots the angry pupil so they get to see the funny side of what is happening, excellent. But if the humour is interpreted as an attempt to belittle in some way, it will be very counter-productive. The element of surprise that a joke can bring to an escalating situation of tension can be highly effective. The key to this strategy is really knowing your pupil well.

Mood matching

There is always a danger that if you adopt a strategy of sounding too calm and detached when a pupil is very angry, your reaction will be interpreted as a lack of interest. If the pupil feels that you are not engaged with their problem, they could get angrier still.

Mood matching is the technique of expressing an interest in what is being said to you – with a level of engagement that appears slightly less than the angry person. This gives them a strong feeling that you really are engaged in what has happened to them. This helps them feel that their problems are going to be dealt with properly.

This strategy carries a high risk. If you get your pitch of mutual concern too high, you could spark them off into another rage.

Active listening

Active listening is an attractive strategy because it implies that you are prepared to take an active role in trying to solve the angry person's problems. It is vital that the angry pupil feels that they have been listened to and their opinions and feelings are being taken into account. At the time when a crisis of rage is pending, it is important to calm down the situation with this promise, an active reassurance to them that there will be a genuine opportunity for discussion at a later point.

You must keep your promise and have that discussion. But it is better to start listening when the incident has truly calmed down and the people involved have cooled off.

I will look at brokering solutions to conflicts in Chapter 8.

HOW TO LOOK AFTER YOURSELF WHEN YOU ARE DEALING WITH ANOTHER PERSON'S CRISIS ANGER

The onset of aggression and anger in one pupil can easily encourage you, the teacher, to **retaliate**. You will think that the pupils expect to see you win a showdown. You will think that your colleagues will expect you to win a power struggle.

But ignore macho culture in schools. Don't retaliate in kind. First, try to avoid getting so angry yourself that you jump headlong into the situation. Watch out for your own warning signals of anger.

Second, de-escalate by trying to depersonalise the situation. Keep on saying to yourself that it is the behaviour of the person, not the person themselves, that you are in conflict with.

Third, remember the key issue. Where possible it is better to give in to a pupil who is on the verge of an aggressive rage than encouraging such an incident to occur by stubbornly sticking to the rules (although, of course, there are some rules that have to be adhered to, i.e. for safety reasons). An outburst of rage will destabilise the learning for everybody in the classroom. So if the pupil is threatening to lose it completely because you are insisting on getting them to take their coat off in your lesson, just leave it for the time being at least.

Macho school culture would scorn this approach and say that the pupil will be getting away with flouting a school rule, while the others see you giving in to bullying. But you will have avoided destroying the lesson with an unpleasant confrontation. The consequences of a pupil's non-cooperation can be dealt with later. Most of the class will be able to understand this as taking a different type of firm stand.

In the medium term when the flash point is passed, the issue can be taken up again. The confrontation can be postponed to a time when there isn't a large class sitting in audience. You can pick your own time for challenging a pupil. The balance of forces will have changed and you will have the support of your colleagues and the behaviour programmes of the school if you need them.

Finally, remember it is OK to feel bad when you have been abused by an angry pupil. It may have been good tactics to brush it off at the time, to ignore it or deliberately minimise the conflict. But it is also totally human to have many negative feelings as a result of what has happened. After difficult situations you may have to take care of yourself in a similar way I advise pupils to, on page 121. That may mean offending macho culture that says teachers should ignore their feelings and keep a stiff upper lip. You must talk to your colleagues and unburden yourself about how you are feeling.

Chapter 8

Dealing with crisis behaviour

So far we have discussed strategies which might stop the anger cycle building up to bursting point. We have looked at ways of conciliating and mediating after a rage has taken place. Despite the best practice, there will be emergencies created by a sudden blow up. How should you deal with an eruption of pupil rage? How do you protect yourself, other pupils and the angry person from their own aggressive destructive tendencies?

ANGER AT THE CRISIS POINT: DOS AND DON'TS

Dos

1 Stay controlled. Show a lower degree of emotion than the person who is in a rage. Total calm may make them worse as the urgency and vibrancy of their mood needs a measured acknowledgement from you. (See mood-matching section, p. 64.)
2 Stay rational. Talk, giving firm clear directions. 'Stop that now. Put it down' may need to be repeated in the same calm voice.
3 Keep talking.
4 Make sure you locate yourself near to an exit or escape route.

5 Keep your distance. Give the violent, angry person plenty of space.

6 Call for help or send a pupil to get it. Tell the angry pupil that you are calling for help so that you can support them in getting control of themselves again.

7 Remove any audience if you can.

8 Instruct other people away from the potential danger. Get sensible pupils who can help you do this involved in carrying out your commands.

9 Get any potential weapons out of the way.

10 Talk to them side by side with your hands behind your back. This helps to create space. Also, standing side on rather than head on diffuses confrontation.

Don'ts

1 Don't use aggressive and confrontational body language.

2 Don't try to make long eye contact with the distressed person.

3 Don't use provocative language, such as 'Snap out of it.' 'Stop being so silly.' 'How old are you?'

4 Don't use physical restraint unless all attempts to calm have failed and the person has become a danger to their own personal safety and/or that of others. (The school's Code of Practice must always be adhered to with regard to physical restraint; see below.)

SCHOOL BEHAVIOUR POLICY

A good School Behaviour Policy should have emergency plans to deal with a crisis of anger and a Code of Practice for guidance on using physical restraint. This is a legally sensitive issue and you must safeguard yourself. The DfEE Circular 10/98

'Section 550A of the Education Act 1996: The use of force to control or restrain Pupils' gives clear guidance; you are advised to refer to this Circular.

Staff will need to know what to do and who they can send for to help them. Pupils with emotional behavioural difficulties in the throes of a personal crisis are likely to respond best to self-assured members of staff who have an air of authority about them. **The confidence of others** will help the problem pupil calm down.

A good School Behaviour Policy will

- have an efficient mechanism for getting support to members of staff
- have individual behaviour plans for pupils who suffer from aggressive outbursts
- make sure that all the school staff are aware of what is in them
- train staff to handle individual education plans sensibly
- show staff how to record an incident properly
- have a way of getting parents involved in the follow-up to the incident
- stipulate who to go to in the school to take a lead in multi-agency involvement in a particular pupil
- have guidelines on physical intervention in line with local education authority policy (unless the school is independent)
- have advice on how an incident can be debriefed effectively to allow time for all sides to calm down and rebuild relationships.

PHYSICAL INTERVENTION

If a pupil is having a violent outburst and is a danger to themselves and/or others, some form of minimal physical intervention may need to be used *as a last resort*, but only if all attempts to calm the pupil have failed. Physical intervention **should**

- be used in line with the School's Behaviour Policy
- be used in the angry pupil's and other pupils' best interests or for the teacher's own personal safety, **not simply as a way of coercing a pupil into what you want them to do**
- involve the use of reasonable force and minimise harm to the pupil
- be used in a way to encourage the pupil to regain control of themselves
- be stopped as soon as a pupil has been shown to have calmed down.

Physical intervention **should not**

- be used as a punishment
- be used to force them to stay in a room for your detention.

After it has been done, a written record should be kept by those involved and those witness to it. Parents should be called in and all aspects of the intervention should be discussed.

You should be aware of the legal implications of using physical restraint and check these out very carefully via your headteacher, LEA and union representative.

The aftermath of a physical intervention

It is my direct experience that an incident such as this leaves the enforcers and the restrained feeling drained both physically and emotionally. People involved will need time to calm down and relax a bit. They need to examine what happened and why it happened. Relationships will need rebuilding and that means exploring the feelings of those involved. (Debriefing will be dealt with in more detail in Chapter 9, 'After the rage is over'.)

Most schools will find it very hard to pick up the pieces after a serious incident where physical restraint has been necessary. The main reason for this is their fear that the school's authority will have been undermined too much by a situation where a pupil has had to be physically restrained. There will usually have been an audience for all or part of the incident. Pupils will go back to parents and tell them what they have seen. Many teachers will also be worried about the effect that an assault on senior managers will have on staff morale. Some will truly believe that it will encourage other pupils into copy-cat action. Unless there are mitigating circumstances, it is unlikely that a pupil will display such outbursts more than a couple of times before indefinite exclusion would beckon.

Schools are also fearful of parent reaction. Fathers and mothers are understandably concerned about violence posed by one disturbed individual. Schools know they have responsibilities for the health and safety of pupils and staff and may wish to skip anger management strategies with a pupil whose disruption they really fear and go straight to the solution of excluding them permanently. They have to consider their public image in the eyes of the media. Violence in schools always attracts their attention and a bad story may have sudden and dramatic effects on the following year's pupil intake to the school.

Chapter 9

After the rage is over

You can get the person to listen *properly* only when the rage is over. No meaningful dialogue can take place during the crisis. Any attempts to do so will probably prolong the angry outburst or provoke another one.

Until the rage has subsided, the main objective has to be to calm the pupil down. (Look back over Chapter 7 to find strategies to best suit individual situations.)

HOW TO DEAL WITH THE OUTBURST OF RAGE ONCE CALMNESS HAS BEEN RESTORED

Rage has taken place because the pupil felt threatened or attacked in some way. Their strong surge of energy took place at a time when they believed themselves to have been unfairly treated, devalued or humiliated.

Rage took place because there was a breakdown in constructive communication. Maybe the pupil has been treated badly, maybe the offence against them is imaginary or completely exaggerated. What is certain is that the pupil has not been able to express how they feel assertively. The only way they have found to show the way they feel is to explode into a rage.

The only way forward now that calmness has returned is for the teacher to try to open channels of rational communication. It is at this stage that the skill of active listening (mentioned on pp. 64–5) is essential. It may have been a skill which could have diffused a situation at Stages One or Two of the anger cycle. But at this stage no further progress can be made without engaging it.

As the conciliatory teacher you must

- just listen and accept
- try to solve the problem that led to the rage
- set out the consequences of an unacceptable outburst of rage.

Just listen and accept

1 Let the pupil speak and have their say.
2 Value the information they are giving you, even if it is at a divergence from what you feel is the true situation, and **especially** if it is at loggerheads with the institutional norms you are supposed to be upholding as a teacher in a school.
3 Show them by your response during the listening process that you have understood why they have been very angry.

Try to solve the problem that led to the rage

1 Use objective non-judgemental questioning about the exact reasons for the angry outburst. What happened? What did they say and do? What did the other people involved say and do? How did this make them feel?
2 Summarise back to the person what you think has been said to you. Describe aloud the emotions and feelings you believe they have been telling you about.
3 Try to solve the problem that has caused the pupil's strong sense of injustice. Try to restore a sense of fairness, even if it can be only a temporary one. Look for ways of stopping any events that will be further provocation or triggers to the situation. This is essentially a patch-up holding exercise.
4 In the long term there will need to be work on the way the pupil handles difficult situations. Most will need further

interventions to stop them getting into outbursts in similar situations in the future.

Set out the consequences of an unacceptable outburst of rage

1 Setting out the consequences to a pupil's violent and abusive outburst is best left for at least a couple of hours after the incident.
2 Use words like 'consequences' rather than 'punishment'.
3 During the immediate aftermath of the outburst it is safe to let a pupil know only in a very neutral way that there will be some consequences to follow the unacceptable behaviour, but the details will be left until calmer circumstances prevail.
4 When the pupil is calmer and more rational, they will be more likely to understand and accept that the consequences of their actions are fair.

In secondary schools, where everybody is in a terrible hurry and where the day is punctuated by frequent lesson changes with one subject teacher following on from another, there is always the temptation to jump in with punitive sanctions too quickly as a knee-jerk reaction. The macho punishment culture that I have mentioned rushes to assert itself. A senior colleague in the hierarchy jumps in feet first. They deal out punishment with emotional theatrical flourish and often the situation erupts again.

When punishment is rushed like this, it is likely to have *only* a negative reinforcing effect on the pupil. If the issues around the incident are brushed aside and the pupil is not listened to in any way, the punishment will be seen as unfair. Making a fresh start in the future will be more difficult as the pupil's ingrained resistance to the school system is likely to become more entrenched. **All too often officialdom put all their energy into shouting a pupil down and shutting them up.** This may seem a neat solution but it seldom deals with the real conflicts of the situation.

There is little work in most of Britain's secondary or primary schools to help pupils learn how to control their own vengeful anger and express their feelings better. In Part 3 of this book I shall outline a specific anger management course which I have piloted in secondary schools.

Before that, you might wish to consider other strategies your own school could use to handle angry situations better. The sensible starting point for this is to see if you have a real policy on behaviour and anger management.

Chapter 10

Whole school approaches to anger management

NOT JUST ONE WRITTEN FOR INSPECTORS

If behaviour is to be managed well, teachers should be involved in revising the school's statements regularly. Some teachers distrust policy documentation, so involving them can encourage ownership of a policy, and implementation.

BEHAVIOUR POLICIES: THE MUSTS

1 It must be a working document that informs everybody's practice, not a document for the archives.
2 It must be taken back to the staff regularly to see if it is working. This is not a waste of energy but a vital way of refocusing everybody on how they can best help themselves and each other.

A good school behaviour policy keeps on asking questions

1 Do we have the right kinds of rewards and sanctions to encourage good behaviour and discourage bad?
2 Is everybody following the systems that have been agreed? How can this be checked regularly?
3 Are the personal, social and health education (PSHE) programmes in the school effectively encouraging better

behaviour? (For example social skills training can include assertiveness or anger management.)

4 Are those social skills reinforced in all the subject lessons pupils go to?

5 How does the school handle crisis anger and confrontation? (What are the contingency plans for dealing with disruptive behaviour, verbal abuse, bullying and fighting? Do all the staff, governors, pupils and parents understand and share the principles on which the school tackles friction between pupils and pupils and teachers?)

6 Is anger management an *explicit* strand of behaviour management in the school? (In most schools, there is plenty of anger but very few schools do much about reducing it. Instead they expect that children will simply conform to basic school rules. They have not worked out a way to react to pupils or teachers with problem anger. They have given no thought to explicit ways of teaching *all* children how they can manage their own anger and other people's better in school. Few if any staff have expert training in how to create or contribute to individual behaviour management programmes or to look at the key issues of anger management.)

7 Are staff taught strategies for minimising and avoiding confrontation/aggression when it does occur? What strategies does a school recommend using? How does the school management reinforce the need to use them? Does the school management lead by example?

WHOLE SCHOOL TACTICS FOR DEALING WITH ANGRY PEOPLE

In Part 3 of this book I shall outline a specific anger management course I have piloted in a school. It is a combination of a number of strategies commonly used to manage anger. But as a teacher you may first want to consider other school-wide strategies that would make a significant difference to the anger levels in your school. These are some of the strategies which would help.

Organising specific training for all the staff

The first strategy is to do with making sure that all the staff have specific kinds of training:

1 Training on understanding the stages in the anger cycle, described on pp. 54–6.
2 Training on some of the classroom strategies already discussed, which they can use to defuse anger, once the cycle has been activated. They are techniques most likely to give them a chance of stopping a confrontation becoming a full blown crisis.

Classroom strategies included:

- Extinction or intervention
- Distraction (for pupil or teacher)
- Relocation (of pupil or teacher)
- Changing (various things)
- Mood matching
- Active listening.

---

3 Training in mediation techniques after a serious confrontation has occurred, so that they are skilled at reaching a constructive compromise which is fair to both sides (either pupil to pupil or pupil to teacher).

Re-examining behaviour modification training regularly

Accept that training on behaviour modification is something which is *never* a one off. It has to be returned to in a major way every year and re-examined afresh. It is at the core of relationships and interactions in a school. It is therefore at the core of the learning process. You will have to persuade your school to put it on the agenda as a major item every year.

Teaching pupils how to behave better

It is not enough to train teachers in how better to handle difficult situations with pupils. The pupils themselves need to be taught how to be better behaved. In particular, they need to be aware of what to do to help themselves when they feel incredibly angry. This will inevitably mean raising their awareness of aggressive macho traditions which often hold such sway within secondary schools, giving them sufficient knowledge and confidence to challenge the stereotypical behaviours they are encouraged to conform to.

A good behaviour management policy *which is put into practice* will be the heart of a school's ethos. There are a selection of programmes that have been used to teach pupils to behave better. In the next section we shall examine them briefly.

ASSERTIVE DISCIPLINE

Assertive discipline is a systematic and structured programme which is designed to give pupils clear, sensible and consistent messages about what is expected of them. The emphasis is very much on the positive – through rewards and verbal praise – but with a series of sanctions that can also be used if necessary.

Assertive communication: teacher to pupil, pupil to pupil

1 **Say what you mean, mean what you say.** Be prepared to repeat the request calmly and sensibly up to five times. Make it clear what you want – personally, directly and within a positive framework. 'I want you to take your coat off now. Thank you for doing that' works much better than 'Why do I have to waste my time telling you to get your coat off? Why can't you do anything you are told without a big fuss? You will stay back ten minutes after school until you can learn to do as you are told.' It is also sensible to use

positive non-verbal communication to back up and reinforce what you are actually saying. Hand movements downwards will encourage calm. Use a head shake for 'no' or a nod for 'yes'. You cannot give yourself confident body language when you are not feeling confident. But you can be aware of your posture and try to avoid situations when you frequently find yourself expressing defensive body language.

2 **Try to catch pupils when they are being good and doing something right.** It is much more effective than noticing them only when something is going wrong.

3 **Use rewards and praise liberally.** Lots of verbal praise can be reinforced through a low-level system of stamps, stickers, certificates and so on. The majority of the class should experience this as a regular routine.

4 **Use sanctions but only after you have given pupils clear warning** that not complying with requests will lead to a negative consequence.

Punishments should be made very explicit in advance of giving them out. They should be in a series of small steps downwards rather than a sudden sheer drop into the pit. For example:

- Infringement – first verbal warning.
- Second infringement – second verbal warning. Pupil's name is written on the board.
- Third infringement – third verbal warning. Pupil's name is underlined. This will result in a ten-minute detention or letter home to parents.
- Fourth infringement – pupil sent out to a senior teacher or a backup colleague in another class.

The exact details do not matter as there are many ways of making sensible systems. What is important is that there is a series of steps and at each stage pupils have the chance to reconsider the consequences and go no further.

Golden rules

You will get further with challenging pupils using positive reinforcement and praise than with constant punishment. But you must be prepared to use punishments when absolutely necessary. Reward and praise are not always possible even if they are always desirable.

To steer a boat you have to be able to steer the rudder to the left (reward) and to the right (sanction), or else you would just end up going round in circles. At the moment teachers are much more likely to end up circling the spot by steering right all the time!

When making a negative point to a pupil, it will often be better accepted if you use PNP: a *positive* comment followed by a *negative* observation, backed up by a *positive* remark again.

Whatever the system of praise and reward that you and the school decide on, it should be one which is a low-level, high-frequency reward, and one which is not too time consuming to maintain. It should be one which leads by a series of small steps to a reward that the pupils really want to have.

Schools that work hard on training teachers in assertive discipline, and give them a good rewards and sanction system, really help them set clear boundaries for pupils with anger management problems. Teachers will handle difficult situations better when they know they have a good system in which teamwork is used to overcome behaviour problems. The more confident the teacher feels about the range of strategies at their disposal, the less prone to tension, frustration and angry outbursts they will be. The assertive discipline will undermine the macho management systems in a school and leave many staff with other choices of how to manage behaviour.

The same range of skills can be taught to pupils who are trying to resolve conflict with other pupils. Teaching the pupils how to be assertive means that you give them the means to express how they feel without resort to verbal and physical abuse of others.

It is a very common situation for one pupil to take another's bag. An assertive response to this, even if not as polished as this one, might be:

'Taking my bag without asking me is making me very angry.'

All too often the response will be an angry one in form of a shouted insult such as this one:

'Give me that you X . . . X . . . !'

Making teachers and pupils more assertive will cut down on situations of aggression in school which sustain the macho culture. There will be fewer attempts to **win or dominate** conflicts rather than **diffuse** them.

CONFLICT RESOLUTION

Being assertive is a good way of avoiding conflict, but in itself it will not always be enough. Pupils and teachers need to know how to handle themselves when a conflict has occurred and both sides want to stop it turning into a drawn-out crisis.

Conflict resolution, like assertive discipline, is best taught as part of the PSHE curriculum. It has to be a plank in the school's behaviour management policy for *all* pupils in the school, not just the ones with unhealthy anger. Every pupil needs to know how to sort out a conflict and dispute.

Explicit principles underpinning conflict resolution

1 Every person has the right to have their own point of view.
2 Try to understand how others feel; try to put yourself in their shoes.
3 Try to get what you want and have your needs met, without hurting the best interest of another person.

4 Look for a solution to a problem in which everybody can come out as a winner. This is sometimes called the win/win scenario.

Some guidelines to solving conflict positively

1 Admit that you have done something wrong and made a problem worse. Acknowledging that you are part of the problem, even in a small way, will help to create a real dialogue from which a solution can be found. Pupils are often disarmed by the teacher who is honest enough to say that they have made a mistake and apologise for it, even if it is only for a tiny part in a chain of events.
2 Wait to resolve a conflict until the angry outburst is at least forty-five minutes old. People's bodies need time to calm down.
3 Use clear 'I' messages about how the things that have happened have made you feel. This is much more effective than blaming others for what has taken place. For example:

> 'Your shouting out in class upset me. I think it is damaging your chances of a good grade as well as everybody else in the class'

is much better than

> 'Don't you care how much you are spoiling my lesson! You are stopping everybody from learning.'

4 Try the 'look at it from another person's point of view' strategy. Ask the pupil to put themselves in another person's shoes and imagine how they would feel. This could help break the selfish obsessive viewpoint they may have on the matter.
5 Personalise the problem. When pupils are trying to evade personal responsibility for something that has gone wrong,

they will try to shift accountability to the whole class and lose themselves in it. For example:

'It wasn't just me. Everybody was mucking about and talking. Why are you picking on me?'

But you can refocus them on their own role by reminding them that their education is a personal journey and pointing out to them that they have an individual relationship with you as their teacher.

'I don't care if other people were mucking about and talking. It does not make what you are doing any better. You won't be able to blame a poor grade on what others were doing in the lesson. You need to stay on task and accept that you are the only one who can have a good lesson for yourself. And if you help me by showing a good example, then I will be able to get on and deal with anybody else that is mucking about.'

There are obvious flaws in this logic if they were stubborn in following them up. For most pupils, the argument that they cannot hide behind communal blame for their own personal future is powerful enough to get them to rethink their position.

6   Try to work through solutions to the problem together. So it is at least in some way a shared activity. The more the solution gives something positive to everybody, the better. Creating a **'win/win'** scenario for both sides is vital.

7   Keep it private. Solve a conflict away from an audience of pupils or other teachers; you don't want yourself or the pupil performing to the gallery. However, you must ensure that you are never alone with a pupil.

PEER MEDIATION

Using pupils to solve the problems that other pupils are having with each other is a very useful behaviour management strategy. The course that I describe in Part 3 of this book relies on this method. On this course pupils work in small groups. They join the group at different times, meaning that there are junior (new) and long-established members. Some of the best learning experiences in the group come from the observations on how to handle yourself better from the more experienced members. Their creditability as peer group is very high. If they hold high position in the macho peer league in the school and advise somebody to give up violence, the message is much more powerful than when it comes from me.

Not all schools can arrange for angry pupils to work in a small group with a teacher. There are other ways in which ordinary pupils can help mediate situations for pupils with unhealthy anger. Like the teachers, they need to be trained in the basic principles of conflict resolution before they start.

Training in the principles of mediation

Before the conflicting sides get together:

1 Teach the importance of being a good listener. Practise the active listening skills we have looked at in Chapter 7 and look at again in the anger management course in Part 3.
2 Make sure that the listener shows that they have heard and understood what each side in the dispute has said. This can be done by repeating the story to the person speaking.
3 Give everyone an equal chance to say their piece and give their version of the story.
4 Stay neutral. Sit on the fence and don't take sides.
5 As soon as you have sorted out exactly what the conflict between the two parties is about, then try to get both the pupils to work together to find a solution which is fair to both sides.

6 It may be better to interview the pupils away from others in the first instance so you can work out what each position is. However, you must ensure that you are never alone with a pupil.

The next stage of a successful mediation is to bring the parties together.

Each person involved in the dispute needs to be able to talk and listen without being interrupted. Before the mediation starts, the pupils need to agree to this rule. They also have to agree that they will abide by solutions that they work out together and genuinely try to find a positive solution to their problems.

The mediator needs to get

• each side to describe the exact problem and conflict to the other
• each side to look at possible solutions
• both parties to pick a solution that both sides can live with
• both sides to check that they know what they have to do to make the solution work
• both sides to look at ways in which they can avoid similar types of problem in the future.

Finally the mediator will try to finish a session positively by praising both sides for coming to a mature and sensible solution (the win/win scenario we have already mentioned).

TRAINING PUPILS IN HOW TO COEXIST HARMONIOUSLY WITH EACH OTHER

The behaviour management policy of a school will also need to outline the ways in which pupils are expected to behave. This can be done through the PSHE curriculum and reinforced by teachers in their daily classroom interaction.

Many students will need training in specific social interaction skills. In my experience one of the most effective ways of doing this is through drama and role play.

Key social skills that need explicit reinforcement

1 Ability to introduce themselves and their ideas orally in a group setting.
2 Good listening skills.
3 Learning how to use eye contact and bodily gestures to help them when speaking.
4 Good turn-taking and teamworking skills.
5 Sharing ideas and equipment.
6 Following reasonable instructions.
7 Ignoring distractions and provocation.
8 Expressing their views and ideas without abusing others.
9 Knowing how to ask for help.
10 Knowing how to receive praise.

These key social skills underpin every aspect of the curriculum. If they are taught explicitly through the School Behaviour Policy, they will help to reduce dramatically scenarios in which there are terrible incidents or rage and anger between pupils and pupils and staff. All teachers have to play their part in making this happen. **Every teacher needs to stress these strategies in their subject lessons and not just in PSHE.**

Part 3

The Everyman project

The inspiration for the pilot anger management course in schools

Chapter 11

The principles of the course

THE EVERYMAN PROJECT

The Everyman project was a South London course run for men who had been violent and abusive to their partners and children in the home. It was a project that I was personally involved with for about nine months. I quickly saw important parallels with the school situation. Many of the individuals on the course justified their verbal and physical violence by blaming others for provoking it. Others justified their behaviour by citing important macho principles of honour, revenge and respect. I could see that the principles and the strategies used on the course had the potential for transfer into schools.

Fraught relationships with school peers and teachers are the same for angry pupils as family relationships were for the angry men of the Everyman course. No doubt relationships within the family would also have had great significance for my angry school pupils but I chose to concentrate my adapted course on the active dynamics of the relationships of the school day.

I transferred and modified the principles of the Everyman project to suit the needs of pupils in my pilot anger management course in the school.

THE BASIS FOR THE PILOT ANGER MANAGEMENT COURSE IN SCHOOLS

Principle 1: taking responsibility for oneself as an individual and accepting that there is always a choice about what one does

The pupils in a school who have been referred for outbursts of verbal abuse or have gone further to physically abuse others need help in understanding that it is both desirable and possible that they can change their behaviour. They are introduced immediately to the idea that it is they themselves who are responsible for what they do. **There is always a choice**: the choice to escalate a situation and engage or to back off from a situation of dangerous abuse.

At one level the work with the pupils has tried to give them direct action strategies to help them control their verbal abuse and violent behaviour. The key techniques are Time Out and the Six Foot Rule, if all else has failed. These are crude but effective behaviour intervention strategies. They will be discussed later in more detail.

But behaviour intervention strategies don't go any way to address the underlying problems of what the pupils are thinking and feeling when they get angry. They need to understand more about what is triggering their verbal abuse and violence.

Role play was used to begin to unpick some of these issues. We looked at re-enacted situations where the pupil had escalated a situation rather than defused it. Such role play shows the point at which the choice to engage or back off takes place. The pupil or groups of pupils involved can look at the motives that led to engagement rather than retreat. This kind of role play will highlight personal attitudes which some pupils have which are sexist, racist, controlling and destructive. It is the teacher's chance to take these up and challenge them.

Principle 2: empathy

Pupils who revert quickly to verbal and physical abuse usually find it very difficult to develop a sense of empathy with others. Yet this is essential if they are to stop behaving abusively. Empathy is the ability to resonate with the way that someone else is feeling.

As the Everyman project so aptly sums up:

> Without empathy we can only treat others as objects rather than as persons, and violent behaviour towards others is usually preceded by the objectification of those others.

Yet angry pupils have great difficulty in seeing the teacher or the fellow student they have just blown a fuse with as a human being. This is a very pronounced feature of almost all angry boys and a significant number of angry girls.

The macho style described earlier (see pp. 33–6) makes it especially difficult for angry boys to deal with their anger as they are already very poor at handling their feelings. Many boys have difficulty in expressing emotion to themselves, let alone to others. If they are uncomfortable about empathising with themselves, then it makes it even harder for them to empathise with others. The behaviour of men on the Everyman project had uncanny similarities to the behaviour of many boys in school. They don't talk about feelings and emotions and have a limited awareness of their own feelings until they have boiled up to extreme or intense levels.

Male culture demands that you show you are hard. Boys grow into men without having a mode of expression to acknowledge fear or grief. Instead they have a great deal of embarrassment and shame connected to these kinds of feelings. **The one kind of emotion that they can express is anger.** This is considered manly. Perhaps the use of the word 'anger' needs a more careful definition. The anger that is often shown is an intense and muddled combination of feelings that have not been worked out properly. They often include a mix of grief, frustration, despair, fear and desperation. The anger is better described as rage and it carries with it a lot of aggression, threat and the wish to hurt and damage others. It is in essence vengeful.

Think of the anger of the more challenging pupils in your classroom. Do some of them struggle to express some of the above emotions as they interact with their peers and each other? Do their disputes often spill over into vengeful behaviour? How often does the teacher have to prevent a pupil getting back at somebody who has insulted or cussed them in some way? Do your lessons have their momentum spoilt by these kinds of disputes and tensions?

The macho tradition also encourages posturing in this form. Young men are encouraged to puff themselves up and pretend to be in a rage. There is a ritual in male anger. It is symbolised perhaps by two boxers staring at each other, about three inches from the other's face in the weigh-in before a fight. But the lines between posturing and the real thing can get easily transformed with the one suddenly becoming the other in a school classroom where a large amount of insecure adolescent egos are interacting.

Principle 3: vulnerability

The pilot anger management course in schools also worked on getting pupils to empathise with their own feelings and those of other people around them. To do this, they often had to drop the hard man image and accept that they were vulnerable. Their rage needed deconstructing so that the emotions underneath could be classified and acknowledged. In particular, pupils (the vast majority of them boys) had to accept that sometimes they feel fear, panic, anxiety, despair, sadness and frustration. And that these feelings are painful. They needed to start to explain these feelings to others by saying, 'I feel really upset when you keep on taking my pencil' rather than 'I am going to beat you up for taking my stuff you X . . . X . . . !' Expressing their anxieties rather than hiding them away would reduce outbursts of aggression and threatening behaviour.

Key aim of the pilot project

The key aim of the pilot project was to get angry pupils to become more emotionally aware. To do this pupils often had to start accepting that there were situations in which they feel vulnerable and that the vulnerable feelings could not be covered up by verbally or physically abusing somebody else. Bullying, intimidating or injuring another person was not going to resolve 'feeling bad' inside yourself.

As far as it is possible we try to show pupils that feeling bad like this is sometimes a part of just being a human being. It is inevitable, natural and has to be lived through. But although it is intensely uncomfortable, it is better to feel like this than humiliate, frighten and injure another person.

VIOLENCE AND ABUSE AS A VICIOUS CIRCLE IN FAMILIES

Many angry pupils may themselves be the products of angry and violent parents, experiencing a lot of verbal and physical abuse in their earlier childhood. It is beyond the scope of the anger management project to delve into this but if it comes up in group discussion or is already known about in pupil case history, then it is a significant factor to bear in mind. In this way the pilot anger management course in schools differs from the Everyman, which seeks to delve deeper into individual history through one-to-one counselling.

A common factor of those who have experienced anger and abuse in their families from an early age is to find it so embarrassing or shameful that they deny or minimise its importance. Boys especially seem to condition themselves to it as a natural way of life. It is so much a part of the culture that they grow up in and the images they see on the television and in newspapers.

As the research on the Everyman course has shown, the men there do not seem to acknowledge that the ill treatment they had as children was damaging or hurtful. Instead they explain it as violence that was necessary to keep them in line and that they often deserved it. The feelings of pain, resentment, powerlessness and shame that must have accompanied the violence and abuse have long been repressed or shrugged off.

Obviously an anger management course in schools needs to help pupils understand their own feelings but also understand the feelings others might have when they are the object of verbal or physical abuse.

THE ALPHABET OF SUCCESSFUL ANGER MANAGEMENT

A – Accept responsibility
B – Be aware of your own warning signs
C – Commit to backing off
D – Deal with your vulnerable feelings
E – Empathise with others
F – Feedback

A–C are dealt with in Module One (see Chapter 12)
D–F are dealt with in Module Two (see Chapter 13)

Chapter 12

Responsibility, choices and action: Module One

LEADING QUESTIONS FOR MODULE ONE

1 Can I take responsibility for myself?
2 What am I doing when I get into trouble?
3 How do I know when I am getting angry?
4 What can I do to stop myself getting out of control?

These four questions have been the core of the pilot anger management course; they deal with the emergency action which is necessary to make a pupil safe so that situations are less likely to escalate. But on their own they are quite a superficial intervention and are unlikely to effect great change unless that pupil's personal feelings during rage are also worked on. Anger management courses have to begin somewhere and starting with the most profound but important principles are good as long as you don't expect the penny to drop immediately.

SESSION 1: CAN I TAKE RESPONSIBILITY FOR MYSELF?

A – Accept responsibility

Key concepts

- Accepting responsibility.
- Responsibility gives choice.

Rationale

The concept of responsibility must be presented first and is probably one of the hardest to accept for many of the pupils who come on the course. They have a strong tendency to blame others in all situations where they are losing their temper. The most commonly used phrases will be: 'It wasn't my fault.' 'They were trying to wind me up.' 'He made me angry.'

Accepting responsibility is a core concept and almost every situation will have to be examined in the light of it. It will be returned to again and again. Events will have to be reinterpreted in terms of accepting responsibility on a regular basis.

Within the concept of accepting responsibility is the pupil's acceptance that he or she has been violent and verbally abusive in the past. The pupil needs to accept that there is always a **choice** whether to be violent or verbally abusive and that the choice is something that the angry pupil **always** has. Also accepting responsibility implies that pupils must commit or promise themselves to a non-violent path in the future. Given the cultural code that glamorises violence this is a particularly hard concept for many of the pupils to absorb.

Their peers and even some of the adults who surround them will legitimise violence and verbal abuse **in certain situations**. Yet at the core to this anger management course is the ethos that **violence and verbal abuse are never acceptable** and must be avoided at all costs. Violence and verbal abuse always lead to the bullying and attempted coercion of others.

In this first session the pupils were asked to talk through school situations in which they had got into trouble. We looked at the things they had done which were their choice and therefore their responsibility. Then we looked at the part of the chain of events which involved other people choosing to behave in a certain way towards them. I emphasised that this was the choice and responsibility of those others and something beyond the influence of my pupil.

Second chances: lots of chances

It is established very soon in the course that it is realistic to expect that the pupils will **sometimes fail** in their resolve to give up violence and verbal abuse. But the teacher hopes that their successes will become much more frequent than their failures. For the sake of convenience I am going to divide up the work of the pilot anger management course into sessions. A session could be as long as three hours or as short as fifty minutes depending on the amount of pupil input and interaction there are in the discussions. The concepts in a session could probably be covered in one average-length lesson if they are simply taught. But they will take a lot longer if pupils argue a lot about what is being said by the teacher and if they volunteer many of their own ideas and experiences. The group dynamic will dictate whether sessions move quickly or slowly. In many ways the slower the better as this is likely to mean there has been lots of argument and discussion.

Also certain key concepts introduced at the beginning will be part of every later session. In that sense one session is embedded into the learning of the next. They all fit inside each other like Russian dolls. The first session is present in the progress of every session.

SESSION 2: WHAT AM I DOING WHEN I GET INTO TROUBLE?

Key concepts

- Understanding a definition of abuse with examples of verbal and physical abuse.

- Understanding the consequences that abuse has on you and your relationship with others.

Verbal and physical abuse

Verbal and physical abuse need to be classified and often the group will ask questions such as: 'Why is that violent?' or 'That's not abusive, isn't it just sticking up for yourself?' Or the group will make statements like: 'They want me to shout because they are trying to wind me up' or 'She started it.'

We look at the kinds of situations that the pupils get themselves into at school. In much of this session work it is often necessary to prompt them with examples of things that the group leader has done in the past. Also we give them visual prompts by writing the beginnings of lists on the board and getting them to add their ideas.

Here is what a list could end up looking like:

Physical abuse

Pushing, slamming doors, hitting, slapping, holding somebody down, breaking objects like pieces of furniture, kicking things across the floor, 'rushing' in the playground, showing or using weapons.

Verbal abuse

Threatening, getting in somebody's face and shouting a lot, outright cussing, cussing but pretending it is just a joke, blaming others for everything that is going wrong, insulting, name calling, saying somebody else's opinion is rubbish.

Many pupils will find it hard to accept that some of the things on the list such as kicking things or slamming doors are actually acts of physical abuse. The biggest discussion is often around whether it is acceptable to push back or fight back when you are attacked.

With verbal abuse, the arguments centre on whether it is OK to abuse back if somebody is in your face doing it to you. Why should you have to take it?

Rationale

The rationale for attacking all these positions lies in the following key points. Abusive behaviour is any kind of act that harms others by the use of power to dominate their wishes or opinions. If this is done physically, it is an act of violence. It is wrong for you to do it and equally it is wrong for them to try to do it to you. But you choose what you do and they choose what they do. If they make a bad choice and try to dominate you through abuse, you do not help the situation by retaliating in kind. It is important to work with the pupils to discover the ways that they can protect their own interests by being assertive about their rights as individuals.

They need to know how to get help when one of their peers is bullying and abusing them.

Assertive behaviour is an important aspect of this course. At this early stage it is important to help the pupils understand that if they have made a mistake in the way they have behaved, there will always be another chance to do things better next time. Many of the angry pupils that I have worked with find it very hard to accept that they have got something wrong but there will be another chance. They find it very difficult to back down about anything. A key part of them **taking responsibility for themselves** over a period of time is gradually learning to be honest about mistakes and being willing to change.

There are other issues around responsibility that will need to be returned to again and again.

Consequences

The issue of taking responsibility includes recognising that the things that I do as an individual have an impact not only on myself but also on those around me. There are **consequences** to the actions that I take as an individual. Those consequences have effects on myself and others.

Pupils often find it difficult to accept that what they do creates consequences for themselves and others. In the heat of their anger they are no longer able to think ahead. They do not anticipate the effect their actions will have on the teacher or the other pupil they have just attacked verbally or physically.

It is important when talking through the events of the week with them to focus directly on the consequences of certain things that they have done. To encourage them to explain how those consequences are possible without disclaiming their part in the chain of events. To get them to see the points at which they had a **choice** about the way that they handled something.

The importance of short role plays

Looking at **consequence and choice** was a regular theme in role plays that I did throughout the pilot project. One I returned to frequently was the role play of an angry teacher with pupils who are mucking about. I got members of the group to play the various roles. They enjoyed taking all the different parts.

After each role play we talked about what had happened and how each member of the group had felt in their different parts. We talked about how things must feel for both teacher and pupils.

In each case the pupils were given very explicit instructions about the type of misbehaviour they were to engage in. The exercises were brilliant in getting the group to get a feel of other points of view in a difficult situation. Each time a role play was done, we could focus on different things.

In some role plays we focused on the moment when some-body should have backed out of a difficult situation. We also looked at the key role of bystanders and got pupils to play their parts. The group gained useful insights into how some of their peers could wind up situations and exaggerate them so as to encourage a fight or a serious bout of verbal abuse. **Often the members had not realised just how much they were being manipulated.**

SESSION 3: HOW DO I KNOW WHEN I AM GETTING ANGRY?

B – Be aware of your own warning signs

Key concepts

- Warning signs give you a signal that your anger is rising.
- They can come in different forms but you have to be on the look-out for all of them.
- You need to be aware of your thoughts, feelings and physical state.

Physical warning signs

Session 3 introduces the concept of the **warning signs** that often lead up to a loss of temper, verbal abuse and violence. We start with the physical warning signs. In all sessions it is vital for the teacher to be brave and honest, leading with examples of what they themselves have done when they were angry and explaining how they have learnt to recognise their own warning signs. This will encourage students to volunteer their own personal experiences. If there is one student who has been in the group longer than the others, they can also be encouraged to take a lead.

I found it helpful to give the pupils a list of things that other people had said had been warning signs for them. This helped them clarify in their own mind what a warning sign might actually be. Here is a typical list of phrases that the group finally came up with:

Muscles tensing.
Heart beating faster.

Faster breathing.
Sweaty palms.
Clenched fists.
Breathing gets hard.
Upper chest goes tense.
I feel tense in my neck and shoulders.
I start rubbing my nose.
I feel myself frowning.
Butterflies in my stomach.
Dry mouth.
I start raising my voice.
I start talking to myself.
Swearing.
Slamming doors.
Blaming others.

Warning thoughts

Psychologists would refer to these as cognitive triggers. What are people thinking as they experience those physical warning signs in their body? Again some personal experiences and anecdotes from the teacher prompt the group and start the list:

I wish you were dead.
I am going to kick your head in.
I'm going to kill you.
It's not fair.
You shouldn't have done that.
How dare you?
It's your fault.
Shut up.
I'll show you.
You're not going to do that to me.
You always do this to me.

Warning feelings

Boys find it hardest to accept that there are emotional triggers
to angry rages. They are often experiencing feelings that they
have never tried to identify properly. At this early point in the
anger management intervention, the issue of emotions is best
touched on superficially. There will be much more exploration
of what the pupils are feeling as the course goes on and the trust
or confidence between teacher and group grows. Also many of
the pupils don't have the literacy and oracy skills to express their
feelings easily in words.

Learning new words for describing **feeling** will become an
educational spin off from the course. But at this early stage a list
of feelings can be made and returned to later:

I feel panic.
I feel frustrated.
I feel like exploding.
I feel disrespected.
I feel that I am being treated unfairly.
I feel trapped.
I feel like bunking off.
I feel different.
I feel sad.

But more than anything the common reply will be:

I feel angry.
To which you will reply:
'What do you mean exactly?'
To which they will reply:
'Angry . . . just angry.'

Many pupils can start to identify the warning signs for anger
in themselves at this stage. But they still have a problem with
taking responsibility for it. They still don't really believe that

they always have a choice about what to do. They continue to blame other people for making them verbally and physically abusive.

Many still relate strongly to macho concepts of honour and retaliation in kind. But the more you engage in work around the detail of what pupils can do about their anger, the more chance that the overall principles will eventually fall into place through **constant repetition and reinforcement.**

SESSION 4: WHAT CAN I DO TO STOP MYSELF GETTING OUT OF CONTROL?

C – Commit to backing off

Key concepts

- Responsibility and choice.
- Certain actions have certain consequences.
- The danger of passing the moment of fatal peril and becoming so angry we no longer have the chance of controlling ourselves.
- The benefits that can be got out of taking a Time Out or staying at least six feet away from another person.
- The constraints that make this difficult.

In Session 4, 'What can I do to stop myself getting out of control?' becomes the key goal. For many of the pupils who attend the anger management course this practical session is easier for them than being asked to deal with the feelings that lead to their spasms of rage.

The moment of fatal peril

This is a useful concept to introduce very early on. It is the split second in which the angry feelings get completely out of control and the fuse which has been lit gets to the dynamite resulting in a huge explosion.

This moment is explained to the pupils as the moment in which they cross from being angry but still capable of doing something about it to when they are shouting and screaming in a complete rage and incapable of listening to any kind of reason until they have calmed down.

The emphasis to **commit to backing off** is that it must occur when the warning signs have been recognised and before the moment of ignition (described as the Stage Three – crisis stage of anger: see pp. 54–5).

Two basic strategies that have been suggested to the pupils are taking a Time Out and observing the Six Foot Rule.

Time Out

Time Outs can be carried out in the playground, a corridor or a classroom. If it is written into an individual education plan (IEP) as a strategy for dealing with anger, a pupil can be allowed to leave a class and go to a particular place and a particular teacher in the school, once warning signs have been recognised.

Good points about using Time Out

1   Time Out in itself can often be a cure to a problem. The pupils who take themselves away from the conflict or confrontation get a chance to calm down and get to grips with the painful feelings that the situation has set off in them.
2   Time Out gives them the chance to think about the consequences of the actions that they were getting themselves into. This is especially useful if they were about to swear at a teacher or have a fight with another pupil. It gives them a chance to get their sense of proportion and balance back and start to rationalise properly again. If they have gone to a teacher who they get on well with, then they may even have a chance to talk through the problem that they have built up

for themselves. The time that elapses may mean that they will be up to going back and sorting out the problem in a different and more constructive way later. It is also likely that the set of circumstances that caused the initial conflagration cannot be repeated again exactly. For example, as is so often the case in schools, the group of bystanders who are busy stirring the situation as much as they can for their own entertainment will not be there next time.

3   Time Out allows tempers to cool on both sides of the dispute, which is also an advantage for the pupil with anger management problems.

Time Out and macho

In my work on Time Outs I stressed a key point that walking away from a situation is not a cowardly retreat. It is in fact the braver of the two options. The macho culture of schools and the society behind them expects and wants to see two pupils give as good as each other in a cussing session. You are seen as a weak pupil if you 'get told' without giving as good as you got. They reinforce the message that walking away from a fight is chicken. And walking away from a fight isn't easy with a large peer group watching at the ringside.

As the group leader, the teacher has to draw out important features of the Time Out for the group to understand. It is likely that they will lead to a lot of arguments as your pupils are going to think that they are being disrespected if they back off. The sort of consequences they almost all find quite persuasive is the danger of being excluded permanently from the school.

Not having the last word is one of the key hurdles you will have to get over with them. It is important to stress that taking a Time Out does not mean that you have lost the argument but that **you have chosen to postpone the argument or not bother to finish it**. Maybe when you come back there won't be anything to argue about anyway. Explaining the Time Out as a brave retreat to the pupils and not as a cowardly way of legging it is vital. This will have to be reinforced time and time again.

Bad points about using Time Out

Teachers who rely on personal domination through verbal dressing downs and sanctions see Time Out as a soft option for the naughty pupil. They will be heard to say:

1 Time Out is taken by pupils who are trying to manipulate the school system.
2 Time Out is taken by pupils who want to get out of a lesson they can't be bothered to work in.
3 Time Out will be used by pupils to show off to their mates about what they can get away with.
4 Time Out gets somebody off being punished for bad behaviour.
5 Time Out for one pupil will encourage others to misbehave and do just as they please.
6 Time Outs undermine the teacher's authority.

In these assumptions the critics are ignoring several important things.

1 The pupil who is allowed to take a Time Out is **different from** other pupils. This is why treating them **differently** is necessary. The majority of pupils will understand this fact more readily than some teachers.
2 This pupil has probably failed comprehensively to respond to being punished again and again. It is time to try something totally different.
3 If it works and the incidents of verbal and physical confrontation are significantly reduced, then surely it was worth it.
4 Why should a teacher necessarily lose face in front of a class if a pupil is allowed to go off to a designated place before an eruption occurs? A teacher is more likely to lose face if they

get into a slanging match with a pupil who then storms out of the room or if they have their lesson interrupted with a fight between pupils.

The Six Foot Rule

Pupils are told to stay at least six feet away from the person they are angry with. If they stick to this distance it is physically impossible to punch or kick another person. They keep themselves out of another person's personal space.

It is better if people back off with a Time Out than hang on and try to practise the Six Foot Rule. But as an emergency procedure, it allows an argument to be sustained and, if kept to, avoids physical violence.

Good points about using the Six Foot Rule

The pupils I have worked with have all liked to test this out through some role play. And it does work. You cannot hit or kick another person from six feet away. You are out of their immediate personal space and if you can't touch them, physical violence is less likely to break out.

Bad points about using the Six Foot Rule

The problem is that it is easy to promise to keep six feet away from the other person until in the heat of the moment you suddenly enter their personal space and get involved in a fight. If a pupil is in danger of having an argument that is going to escalate out of control, then they are best to back off **properly** as it is unlikely that they will be able to control themselves using the Six Foot Rule alone if they pass their 'moment of fatal peril'. For most angry pupils in a confrontation, it is too risky as a strategy. Pupils who keep to the Six Foot Rule would still find themselves in terminal trouble in most schools as they can still shout plenty of abuse at pupils and teachers from within a fifty-foot radius.

SESSION 5: WHY IS IT SO HARD TO BACK OFF?

Key concepts

- Looking at factors which stoke up anger.
- Looking at the times when you managed to avoid getting very angry and compare them to the times when you haven't.

Rationale

It is important that the pupils in the group discuss the feelings they have at the time the crucial decision to back off and take a Time Out has to be made.

Again it is a very useful ice-breaker to talk about an occasion when you as group leader have got into a situation when you have needed to back off and have either succeeded or failed. Then ask members of your group about a situation when they have got themselves in big trouble. What exactly was going through their mind at the time? How were they feeling inside?

This is the kind of list you are likely to come up with. The process of producing this list is very useful to the members of the group as they are fascinated to hear other people describing their feelings.

Why I don't back off

Because I'm right and I shouldn't have to.
It's not fair.
I will feel disrespected.
The others might think I am weak.
The others might think I am wrong.
I always back off, well not today.
I don't care what happens to me.
I want to get even.
I want to teach them a lesson.
I need to have the last word here.

I started this so I will finish it.
I felt I was being tested.

At this stage I get the group to consider what they thought or felt on the occasions they have managed to control themselves and get out of a confrontation situation. We look at their success stories and I add my own if there don't seem to be too many around. One of the benefits of working with a group that has some long-serving members is that they often have very good examples of recent success to tell the others about. Their input is highly effective as they are often pupils with a lot of street cred.

A typical list of success stories

I knew if I got in another fight I would get kicked out of the school.
I knew I was on my final warning.
My Dad will kill me if he gets called up to the school again.
I don't want to kill somebody.
I know I feel bad now, but it will feel worse if I don't back off.
If I back off, it's not the same as agreeing.
I tried it last week and it works.
My Mum will ground me for six weeks if I get in more trouble.
My Mum will cry and she's got enough on her plate at the moment.

Avoiding negative consequences dominates the list. But there are signs in some of the answers that members of the group can consider their own feelings and those of close family. (This awareness will need developing in the later sessions of this course.) Clearly being successful at backing off on some occasions helps people to do the same thing again. They begin to remember how to do the right thing when they find themselves in difficulty.

Chapter 13

Having feelings and learning to live with them: Module Two

LEADING QUESTIONS FOR MODULE TWO

1 How do I feel when I get angry?
2 What sorts of feelings do I have in different situations? Can I label them with words?
3 How can I look after myself when I am feeling angry?
4 What is empathy? Why is it so important to help me manage my anger?
5 How well do I listen to other people? How can I learn to listen better?

SESSIONS 6 AND 7: HOW DO I FEEL WHEN I GET ANGRY? WHAT SORTS OF FEELINGS DO I HAVE IN DIFFERENT SITUATIONS? CAN I LABEL THEM WITH WORDS?

D – Deal with your vulnerable feelings

Key concepts

- Members of the group look inside themselves and try to understand what it means to feel vulnerable.
- They are encouraged to explain how they have felt in both good and bad situations in their lives.

Rationale

Research has shown that many boys find it hard to show their emotions because they are encouraged to be manly. Being manly often means suppressing feelings, especially those of sadness, grief and fear. When emotions cannot be suppressed any longer they burst out as an explosive cocktail of anger and rage. This is the way that a male can get it off his chest. A significant minority of girls have copied this macho approach to dealing with feelings. They also cannot express their emotions assertively but only aggressively.

It is hard to tackle this session without first exploring what the words **being vulnerable** actually mean. It is hard to explore these feelings with a group of boys because vulnerability is taboo. So I start off with a description of the word which attacks some of the presuppositions. (This is adapted for school use from the Everyman project group session materials.)

Being vulnerable means that I accept that I am not good at everything. In fact I have some weaknesses and this means I can feel hurt on some occasions. I don't always have total control over what is going on around me. My parents, teachers, family and friends can have a big influence on my life. And because I don't control everything then there is always the chance of the future bringing some pleasant surprises but also some disappointments. I have to be fair to other people and accept that they are not just there to give me exactly what I want all the time. In fact all other people are my equals – their opinions and feelings have equal importance to my own. If their feelings and opinions are different, then that may be a big disappointment to me but I will have to learn to live with it.

In everybody's life there is going to be good times as well as bad times, joy but also sorrow and pleasure as well as pain. Being human makes it a fact of life that sometimes you feel good, sometimes bad. So feeling vulnerable at times is unavoidable. But when I am feeling terrible, **violence or verbal abuse is not the way to solve my problems**.

I ask members of the group to go through times in their life when parts of the statement on vulnerability may have applied to them. It helps if the teacher or a long-standing member of the group gives an example of each kind of situation to start with as the others are almost certain to feel inhibited about expressing themselves. Start with something that gives positive feelings before going on to things that engender negative feelings.

Some useful scenarios

- Times in your life when you realised you had some talent for something.
- Times when you realised that you were not that good at something.
- Times when you have been happily surprised.
- Times when you have been very disappointed.
- Times when you realised that you were being unfair to somebody else and pushing them around a bit.
- Times when you realised that somebody else had a different view to yours about something but you found it hard to accept.
- Times when you had a really great experience and you felt very good about yourself.
- Times when you were very sad and disappointed about what happened.

Talking about some of these things will be very hard for some members of the group. They may well trivialise or make a joke about their experiences. But stick to the exercise and try to pick out a couple of stories where members of the group are able to describe vividly and honestly how they felt.

School situations

Now ask pupils about school situations when they got into trouble. Question them carefully about how they were feeling about what was happening to them. The word used time and time again is **angry**. But what is this exactly?

Even allowing for the fact that not all the pupils will have a vast range of words to describe what feeling angry means, a list will begin to form. The teacher can use their own experiences to help prompt that process. Here are the kinds of feelings that can be teased out of pupils:

Disappointed.
Disrespected.
Guilty.
Rejected.
Not appreciated.
Confused.
Put down.
Shamed.
Betrayed.
Anxious.
A failure.
Like my feelings don't count.
Stupid.
Let down.
Trapped.

To tease more out of the group, you could tell them a story which clearly isn't one of theirs. Here are some examples:

Tina is new in the class. She has come from a different part of the country. When she arrives in her new class, the other pupils start taking the mick out of the way she dresses and the way she speaks. How do you think she will feel? What might she do next?

They take Steve's hat and stick it down the toilet. He loses his temper and tries to attack one of them in the classroom. How do you think Steve was feeling? What might he do next?

Tim seemed to have all the friends. All the boys liked him because he was good at football. All the girls seemed to fancy him. Tim didn't bother to talk to John. He just ignored him or made rude comments about the way he looked. John really wanted to be his friend but in the end he decided he would fight him instead. How do you think John was feeling? What should he do next?

Every time Christine goes into Mr Brown's lesson, he starts picking her up on her uniform and jewellery. He shouts at her every time she talks to her neighbour. He keeps her in after school to do more work because he says she doesn't do enough in the lesson. How do you think she feels about it? What should she do next?

These case studies provoke some different, more personal responses and help pupils out with words that are closer to the bone. It is easier to be more personal about information which isn't personal to them.

Now we get a list which includes words like these:

Isolated.
Lonely.
Dread.
Sad.

Frightened.
Humiliated.
Weak.
Panicked.
Brushed off.
Judged.
Hopeless.
Persecuted.
Left out.
Jealous.
Hate myself.
Inadequate.
Trapped.
Controlled.

Some groups will be able to come up with these and others themselves but **many will need to have words suggested in a pre-prepared list which they can simply tick if they agree with them**.

As has been said before, some pupils' literacy and oracy skills will not be good enough to understand the meaning of some of these words. A minority will find it very hard to say or tick anything at all. They feel too embarrassed and uncomfortable about being asked to talk about emotions like this.

Using role play

Role play can be very useful (see pp. 102–3). A scenario in this case is taken for one of the group members, Wayne. He came in late to his tutor period and found that Kate was sitting in the place where he usually sits. He decided that he wanted to sit there and tried to force her out of the seat by verbally abusing her. When this didn't work, he picked up her bag and flung it across the room. This *did* get her to move but got him into a very serious confrontation with the teacher.

This incident was part of a series of referrals that I wanted him to talk about with me from the previous week. This one was fresh from that very morning and had a great sense of immediacy about it. As we went through the situation Wayne said he would have punched Kate, only hitting girls made you a poof. But he kept on saying that the form teacher had a seating plan and that made what he did right. We asked for the advice of one of the long-standing members of the group and he said that Wayne should have asked the teacher to sort out the dispute rather than take the law into his own hands. As this advice came from a member of the peer group rather than me, it had the authority of 'real speek'. So then we decided to act it out. Wayne had to be his victim Kate, another pupil played the teacher and I played Wayne.

After they had acted it, I asked them how they felt, while they were still in character. Wayne found it very hard to empathise with Kate. He kept on saying that he did not think she would be that bothered by what he had done.

Then I was able to get Kate from her lesson. I asked her if she felt up to coming to tell Wayne and the group how she had actually felt. (This would not always be an option but on this occasion I reckoned on Kate being a strong enough character to face up to Wayne in the group.) She told Wayne that she had felt very upset by the way he had treated her. She told him that what he had done was out of order.

What was most interesting about what she said was that if he had asked her nicely, she would have moved anyway. This brought Wayne up with a start. He was uncomfortable and embarrassed but he could not deny the feelings she had expressed. He also had to accept that the verbal abuse and bag flinging were unnecessary and saying 'please' might have gone a lot further. In fact a please would have made the intervention of the teacher unnecessary.

This kind of role play gets pupils to unravel their own feelings and begins to deal with the more complex issue of how other people may feel in the situation. If they begin to anticipate the way their behaviour could affect others, they are beginning to show **empathy**, something we shall be dealing with in more detail later in this chapter.

How much role play you decide to do is very much up to you. Role play based on real situations that are fresh in the pupils' memory are very powerful. Role play in which they are asked to take the role of the victim is also very effective.

The technique I used on this occasion of getting the victim to come and speak up for herself may not always be appropriate. But it gave this occasion an added realism.

SESSION 8: HOW CAN I LOOK AFTER MYSELF WHEN I AM FEELING ANGRY?

Key concepts

- Expressing feelings can be uncomfortable.
- Difficult feelings have to be lived through, not ignored.
- Faced with this situation, you need to find ways of comforting yourself.

Rationale

Whether a person works themselves up into an angry rage or is able to take a Time Out and back off, they are still going to have to handle some very difficult feelings, probably some of the ones described in Session 7.

A person in a rage gets into some ugly displacement activity. This diverts them from the feelings they were having before their outburst started. At the peak of their rage they blame others for what is happening rather than face up to the horrible feelings inside themselves. The person who avoids the rage stays with their primary feelings. But they are still feeling groggy inside. When the Time Out has calmed them down, the various feelings that are making them vulnerable have to be given a chance to work themselves through their system. This uncomfortable process can be handled more successfully if a person finds ways of **looking after themselves**.

One of the most important points to repeat constantly to the group is the need to accept that it is OK to feel bad and that it is quite natural to feel like that from time to time in life. Those feelings have to be allowed to pass through your body, mind and spirit. From this will emerge a natural and healthy resolution to the problem whereas lashing out in a rage at somebody else can only compound the misery.

Working out how to take care of myself

When I led group sessions I explained what I did to relax and generally enjoy myself. I then went on to explain how I tried to do some of these things when I was feeling very vulnerable. I also explained what happened if I failed to take care of myself at moments when I knew I was getting to feel very upset. The group were then asked to explain what they did when they wanted to relax and enjoy themselves.

Between us we were able to produce a general list like this:

Talk to a friend.
Talk to someone.
Stroke the cat.
Watch television.
Look at fish.
Go running.
Go cycling.
Listen to music.
Play on my gameboy.
Deep breathing.
Tell a joke.
Look at the sky.
Treat myself to chocolate.
Have a cup of tea.
Do hobbies.
Go to a place which always has good memories.
Give myself a present.

Cut down on the list of things I am supposed to do that day.
Go out and play football.
Go easy on myself.

I also asked the pupils what they could do to take care of themselves within the school environment if they were feeling vulnerable. The terminology that they understood better was feeling angry but I wanted to stress the new words feeling vulnerable, so that they get used to applying such concepts to themselves.

Within the school setting these were the suggestions they came up with:

Talking to a friend who can help me have a laugh.
Going out at break time to play football or basketball.
Laying my head down at lunchtime and having a little sleep in the year base.
Treating myself to an extra pudding.
Listening to my Walkman.
Sending a text message to a friend at another school.
Trying to get away from all other pupils and sit under a tree on my own for five minutes.
Getting my homework done and out of the way so I can look forward to the whole evening off.
Going to play on the computer.
Reading a book in the library.

Some schools will be hard pressed to provide most of the above activities. Many will have more. But school itself is a place where it is difficult to find privacy and escape from peer group pressure.

SESSION 9: WHAT IS EMPATHY? WHY IS IT SO IMPORTANT TO HELP ME MANAGE MY ANGER?

E – Empathise with others

Key concepts

- To try to get pupils to understand what empathy means.
- To try to get them to apply it to situations where they are dealing with other people's feelings.

Definition of empathy

I started by giving the group a working definition of the word empathy.

> Showing another person empathy means allowing myself to be in tune with them. I recognise that they are a human being just like me. It means being aware that others feel sadness, anger, joy, fear, despair, pain and pleasure and their own needs and desires are as important to them as mine are to me. Empathy is my ability to put myself in their shoes, to try to imagine what they are thinking and feeling. This is the basis of all good relationships.

Role plays

In all the role plays that we had done so far we had touched on the importance of empathy. By getting pupils to play the role of another pupil or of a teacher, they were being asked to make themselves aware of the thoughts and feelings of others in a confrontational situation. By talking through various incidents that had happened during the week to each individual the group leader could encourage pupils to empathise with others. So how do you think Ms Cooper felt when she asked you to sit down and you ignored her? What do you think Graham felt when you cussed his sister and Mum? Why do you think Jane shouted back at you like that and flung your pencil case on the floor?

Many of the angry young people will find it very hard to resonate in any way with another person's needs, feelings and motivations. Once they themselves feel vulnerable in some way, they begin to treat the other person not as a human being but as an object over which control must be won. As in the earlier role play exercise with Wayne and Kate about who was going to sit in a particular seat, it is vital to pressure them to consider the feelings and motivations of others.

Hot seat exercise on empathy

In this session I have used a hot seat exercise. Each person is put under the spotlight and asked questions about a particular incident in which they got into a rage and then into a lot of trouble at school. Members of the group are allowed to join in with the group leader in asking them questions about what happened.

Everybody who takes part has the chance to see the incidents from an **outsider's viewpoint**. They can see what somebody else did and where somebody else went wrong. They are given the chance to think about how a difficult situation could have been handled better. When they go onto the hot seat themselves they find they are being asked detailed questions about something they did.

Some of those enquiries will challenge what they have always considered to be acceptable behaviour. The group leader will return to the question of how their behaviour made the people it was directed at feel.

The relentless pursuit of this is a very important part of work in the anger management course group. **The pupils have to be continually challenged to think how their actions make other people feel.** They need to develop their emotional awareness of others. It is often very stunted and needs this constant attention to grow.

SESSION 10: HOW WELL DO I LISTEN TO OTHER PEOPLE? HOW CAN I LEARN TO LISTEN BETTER?

F – Feedback

Key concepts

- Understanding that you have to calm down before you try to sort out a problem.
- There are always two sides to an argument and you need to listen to what another person has to say and compromise with them in some way.

Rationale

Angry pupils find it hard to empathise with others and this stems from the fact that they find it very difficult to **listen** to what other people are trying to tell them. When aroused they are likely to interrupt and shout another person down. The macho culture that influences them also celebrates verbal and physical domination rather than communication between people.

Pair work: teaching pupils how to listen better

Pupils test their own listening skills by experimenting in situations where they are not pressurised by their own anger. Each pupil is asked to speak for one minute about themselves (personal history and hobbies) to a partner. Then the partner is asked to repeat back as much of it as they can to the whole group. It is an excellent test of how well a person concentrated on listening to information about somebody else.

It is quite evident when doing this exercise that many people in the group find it very difficult to concentrate on what their partner has said to them. It is a real struggle for them to take in the information.

Then the pair work is extended into a new and more difficult role play. Two pupils are briefed individually about a dispute they are having. Each is given information about what their own position in it is. What do they want to happen? What do they feel about the situation? Do they feel they have been treated unfairly? Then they are told to make sure they get their position across to the other person.

This exercise should lead to a lot of shouting and interrupting and not much listening.

So what makes listening without interrupting difficult?

The pupils give their opinions:

> I am impatient.
> It doesn't feel right.
> I want to have my say.
> I want to put my side.
> I want to get the last word.
> I get stuck on the way I'm feeling.
> I disagree with what is being said.
> I have heard it all before.
> I already know what he is going to say.
> I don't want to hear it.
> I win the argument if I shout the loudest.
> If I have to listen, they win and I lose.

After the rage is over

After a situation where verbal and/or physical abuse have taken place, pupils will usually need to re-establish a relationship with the people they have had a bust up with. To do this effectively, they will need to learn that the victims of their abuse will probably be suspicious and distrustful of them. They will be fearful of further attempts to bully and intimidate them.

Being able to say you are sorry for what you have done will be a vital way to begin rebuilding that trust. But it is also essential that the abusive person listens to the victim's feelings and opinions now the rage has passed. The two sides need to work together on ways that can avoid a breakdown in communication again.

This **feedback** between the two pupils who have had the confrontation in school is vital so that each can hear the other's perspective in an atmosphere that is not charged with the threat of verbal and physical abuse. In most cases there will have to be a teacher there to make sure that it is conducted successfully.

The same process should apply after a confrontation between a pupil and a teacher.

The more often angry pupils are empowered to take responsibility for resolving problems in a calm fashion after they have previously broken down because of a rage, the better. The more they are able to listen to what other parties have to say and take on board what those other parties feel, the more progress they will make.

SESSION 11: SUMMARISING THE A–F ALPHABET OF SUCCESSFUL ANGER MANAGEMENT

Accept responsibility

You have to own up to the fact that you have been verbally abusive and violent to others in the past. You have to admit that there was always a choice in those situations about what you did. You have to commit yourself to choosing non-violence and verbal abuse in the future.

Be aware of your own warning signs

Your body, mind and emotions will tell you when there is danger. Physical signs include tension in the neck and shoulders, stomach churning or sweat on the palms of your hand. Emotional triggers include the feeling of hurt, not being listened to or panic. Your mind might start thinking in a jumbled way. Thoughts like 'I'll teach you a lesson!', 'You can't do that to me!' or 'Shut up now or I'll shut you up!' Or you could find yourself beginning to behave in a way that you know is aggressive and dangerous, for example shouting in a loud voice, leaning forward into somebody's personal space, finger pointing and raising your fist.

Commit to backing off

If you can pull out of the situation you keep both yourself and the victim of your abuse safe. Standing at least six feet away in an emergency will stop you making physical contact. But better still is a Time Out in which you give yourself enough time and space to do something about the situation.

Deal with your vulnerable feelings

Your body will need time to cool down so that you can allow yourself the chance to experience feelings of being **vulnerable**. Being honest about what you feel and putting a name to it can be very hard but it is important as it will help you understand yourself better. These vulnerable feelings are usually very unpleasant and hard to face up to. Some examples of these feelings are fear, powerlessness, loneliness, feelings of inferiority, failure and so on. At this point you need to think of ways of comforting yourself while these difficult feelings last. Have a list of favourite activities to help take care of yourself, such as watching TV, going out to play football or playing a computer game.

Empathise with others

Try to stay in tune with the feelings of the person you are in dispute with. Remember that, however bad they are making you feel, they are human beings too with their own needs, feelings and motivations. A teacher who shouts at you in front of a class may be feeling scared and tense because of the large audience. A pupil who is rude and unpleasant to you may be worried about their image in front of their friends. If you can keep this in mind, it will stop your confrontation with them getting completely out of hand and make it easier for you to resolve your differences later.

Feedback

After the dispute is over, there will be a need to build bridges and resolve matters. Did you even hear what the person you got into dispute with you was saying? Can you listen properly now? Can you explain what you want them to hear about you, calmly and politely? Are you able to empathise with their situation and try to put yourself in their shoes?

SESSION 12: PUTTING THE PUPILS ON THE TWO-WAY PATH

It is good to end the anger management course by looking at the progress each pupil has made. They can be reminded of the diagram that summarises what they have learned (see p.130).

Using the two-way path model

The diagram which the pupils copy down is an excellent way of summarising the whole course of anger management. But it could also be used differently if it was drawn up much earlier in the course. Pupils could fill it in box by box as they work through each session. In this way the two-way path model would become a visual working document, a bit like an advent calendar with a door that needs opening every day.

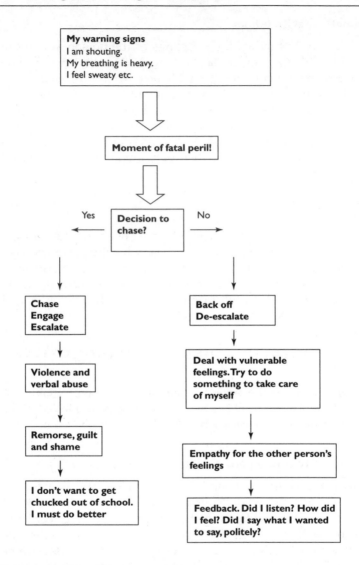

Two-way path model
© The Everyman Project

TWO CASE STUDIES

The anger management course works well for some pupils and not so well for others.

Case study: one that failed

Rob was a statemented pupil. He had a thick Special Needs folder with a long history of arrival and departure from primary schools. He had general learning difficulties which manifested themselves in poor literacy and numeracy skills. But he also had an extensive history of confrontation with his peers and teachers with verbal abuse and some physical violence.

Within a few weeks of coming into secondary school he started to get into violent quarrels with other Year 7 pupils and ugly verbal confrontations with teachers. The problems with the other pupils quickly snowballed into Rob attacking them. The problems with teachers led to him storming out of the classroom.

Once he had worked himself up into a rage there was nothing anybody could say or do that made any difference. He was not able to calm down until he had blown his fuse completely. In the process he would often wander off round the school and burst into lessons. This aspect of his behaviour was very disruptive and got him noticed by a very wide range of pupils and teachers.

In Rob's case the level of rage was simply too hard to contain and work on in a normal school setting. There were deep-seated psychological problems in the way he related to other people.

The programme of anger management I have described failed to work on Rob. He was able to attend only about five weekly sessions before he was excluded from school permanently. When he was in the sessions he seemed to respond well, particularly to an older member of the group who was able to speak with confidence about the improvements the course had made on him. Although this was productive, it was too little and too late. Rob was unable to grasp the key concepts in any meaningful way and apply them to himself. He did not take responsibility for himself and remained oblivious to his own warning signs. He did not commit himself to backing out of difficult situations. Despite some imaginative attempts to help him with his behaviour, Rob was asked to leave the school.

Case study: one in which a lot of progress was made

For Andrew the anger management course was a significant success. It did not transform his personality totally. He still got into arguments and scraps. But 90 per cent of the time he was sufficiently aware of his warning signals to back out of situations in which he might become verbally and physically abusive. He had a better understanding of how difficult situations made him **feel** and the beginnings of being able to empathise about how his actions might make others feel. He had the tremendous advantage of positively reinforcing his own progress by telling other members of the group about his successes.

SPECIFIC INTERVENTIONS

Both the pupils I have described were in many ways extreme cases. They both had statements for behaviour and literacy difficulties. Many pupils who go to anger management sessions need only specific interventions on their abusive behaviour.

All pupils and teachers could benefit from raising their awareness of how to handle confrontation effectively. **Most schools need to calm down the interactions in their classroom, corridors and playground.** Everybody gains from pupils and teachers improving the way they relate to each other.

Chapter 14

Conclusion: the need to promote emotional intelligence

HOW FAR DO ANGER MANAGEMENT AND OTHER BEHAVIOUR STRATEGIES REALLY WORK WITH EMOTIONALLY VOLATILE PUPILS?

Pupils with emotional and behavioural difficulties (EBD) have usually had something go wrong for them when they were younger learners. They may also have suffered trauma in their earlier lives within the family which has affected the critical relationship with key adults at an important time in the learning process. They may have had an illness or physical impairment as a very young child that set them behind their peer group. Whatever the problem, I believe that learning is a deeply emotional experience and that a key to successful learning is the development of secure emotional/intellectual relationships between a child and key adults. If something spoils this for whatever reason, the damage is very hard to reverse later in the school career.

LIMITATIONS TO ANGER MANAGEMENT STRATEGIES

1 Anger management strategies will have very little effect on pupils if they won't admit to having a problem, are not prepared to take responsibility for themselves and continue to blame others repeatedly for what is going wrong. Teachers

using anger management strategies in this situation will be doomed to failure, as all the old offences will repeat themselves.

2 Anger management strategies will also fail if the vast majority of the teachers in the school don't understand them or won't give them a chance. Pupils who are genuinely struggling to improve the way that they handle themselves in difficult situations will need flexibility and compassion from staff, if they are to change positively. There are going to be significant times when they will fail. Their improvements may come in small steps and that fact needs to be recognised and accommodated by the teachers around them.

3 For anger management strategies to make headway, they need to be championed by a small group of dedicated staff **as an absolute minimum**. One residential expert will make minimal progress.

4 Other behaviour management strategies in the classroom such as positive reinforcement and extinction will have significant success with EBD kids. **But they will not make their problems go away completely.** Nerve-sapping irritations of fidgeting, not concentrating and winding up others will still go on in 'modified form'. The bitter reality of inclusion for many EBD pupils is that they can be contained in the classroom only by using good teaching strategies. If bad ones were used, there would be serious disruption and confrontation all day long. Inclusion for the angry pupils themselves is a very positive thing. Through the sheer endurance and imagination of their teachers they are able to benefit from schooling in a normal environment.

But their inclusion for the other pupils in the class is not so appealing. Minimising the difficulties created by EBD pupils keeps many teachers tense and strained. It takes its toll on them mentally, physically and emotionally. The atmosphere of fidgeting, low-level concentration and poor peer group interaction may be kept to a minimum but it still has a great effect on the atmosphere in the classroom.

BENEFITS OF ANGER MANAGEMENT STRATEGIES

1 Disruption from EBD pupils is kept to an uncomfortable minimum.
2 Borderline pupils are much more likely to co-operate with the teacher rather than swing the wrong way.
3 The vast majority of well-motivated pupils gain by a stable classroom atmosphere which cuts down on the amount of confrontation and aggression.
4 The same applies to the anger management course that I have described in this book. Although it was obviously aimed at pupils with specific problems with their tempers, it will probably have more of a dramatic effect on well-balanced pupils as a part of their PSHE programme. It is very useful that *all* pupils gain a framework for understanding their own difficult feelings better. **Schools need to cultivate emotional as well as academic intelligence.** Both are vital for individuals wanting to lead a happy and well-balanced life. It will help *every* young person manage their feelings better when they get into dispute and difficulty with others. At the moment, the system provides them with very little guidance on what to do when they are feeling frustrated and angry.

ANGER MANAGEMENT AND THE CLASH OF CULTURES

In the real world as it is at the moment, anger management will have only limited success in curbing rage and aggression in schools. There is bound to be tension in a school where reading and writing are the tools for progress and success but a substantial proportion of the student population are not good at them.

The cultural traditions which glorify macho male behaviour will resist an alternative school culture which challenges them. It would be foolish to think that all pupils will want to change their behaviour. They won't be easily persuaded that backing away from confrontation or expressing feelings in other ways is the right thing to do.

ZERO TOLERANCE AND EXPLICIT EXPECTATIONS

Confronting macho behaviour is never going to be easy when it has such ingrained cultural power. I feel that a **very clear standpoint** needs to be taken against it and issues cannot be fudged.

We need zero tolerance of physical bullying and verbal abuse. A school behaviour policy should say that pupils must respect each other and specifically declare that 'all hands and feet should be kept to yourself except in situations of contact sports'. **This would give teachers a real lead in stopping physical and verbal confrontation in school. There should also be zero tolerance of any form of cussing or verbal abuse, including the often used argument that it was all just a joke.**

As I described with the lunchtime disruption that I observed (see pp. 24–6), it is from small seeds that big problems grow. The problems need to be challenged effectively before they germinate rapidly.

PERSONAL, SOCIAL AND HEALTH EDUCATION (PSHE)

A PSHE programme which challenges pupil machismo in all its forms and a headteacher who challenges the bullying techniques of a minority of influential staff will begin to make a *huge* impact on the way that relationships in schools support the learning process.

DRIVING UP ACADEMIC STANDARDS AND IMPROVING RELATIONSHIPS

A recent education speech from the government not only admitted that the early teenage years were a difficult time but also talked of tapping into the flood of adolescence by driving up educational standards. While raising standards in numeracy and literacy is very commendable, it can never be the whole answer to the difficulties some teenage behaviour presents. There needs to be a proper study of the subcultures that encourage pupils to behave aggressively. The fact that physical and verbal abuse is 'celebrated' in so many aspects of young people's lives needs to be confronted rather than ignored.

I give you a recent example at the time of writing notes for this book on the train. I was reading a keynote speech by the Minister for Education and his vision for the twenty-first century. All around me people were reading the front page newspaper story of violence in a European football match. In a strange kind of way the two are linked. One has tremendous indirect power to stop the other from happening.

As I have already said, football hooliganism is just one way that macho regularly shows its ugly face. The press condemned it heartily as they always do, yet their cameras formed a ring around a group of violent supporters who taunted and attacked each other. There is endless fascination and awe for macho in sport and many other walks of life.

The negative energies created by such anger has gained a strong hold in the classrooms. It could turn all talk of driving up academic standards into meaningless rhetoric.

I believe we will know when we have a real chance of transforming standards in state education. It will not be when government test results rise a level or two but on the day when verbal abuse and cussing are no longer a monotonously regular feature of pupil interchange in classrooms as they are in some schools now.

Underlying all school improvement is the need to improve the emotional and intellectual relationships between the teacher and the pupils. At the moment there are too many barriers to this. They come from within the schools themselves where some teachers gain their power by bullying the pupils and their colleagues. Bullying which flourishes within the student population itself, where boys are drawn to the rigid macho role models which encourage them to be aggressive and physical, to seek domination and repress their true feelings.

Ironically, the education system of the 1970s and early 1980s recognised the importance of emotional intelligence as a key ingredient of successful education. The more liberal educational establishments of that era put a lot more effort and energy into challenging gender stereotypes and promoting equal opportunities. They placed greater emphasis on the hidden curriculum, a phrase that has all but disappeared from educational terminology. This led to innovative PSHE programmes and lesson materials in many schools. The onset of the National Curriculum swept away much of this valuable work. Driving up standards, teacher performance and school improvement became the watch words for an approach to acquiring knowledge and skills. The cultivation of emotional intelligence became a casualty of this. Undoubtedly there have been key improvements in schools in significant ways as a result of a more prescriptive curriculum, but the prevailing climate has given the macho value system the chance to gain an even stronger foothold than before. The need for anger management courses in schools has never been greater than it is now.